D1478931

ERNST BENZ

CHRISTIAN KABBALAH

Neglected Child of Theology

Translated from the German by
Kenneth W. Wesche
Edited by Robert J. Faas

Library of Congress Cataloging-in-Publication Data

Benz, Ernst (1907-)
[Christliche Kabbala. English.]
Christian kabbalah: neglected child of theology/Ernst Benz;
translated from the German by Kenneth W. Wesche.
p. cm.
Includes bibliographical references (p.) and index.
ISBN 1-59650-000-X (alk. paper)
1. Cabala and Christianity--History--17th century. 2. Cabala and
Christianity--History--18th century. 3. Oetinger, Friedrich Christoph,
1702-1782. 4. Cabala--History. 5. Theosophy--History. I. Title.

BM526.B463513 2004
296.1'6--dc22

2004047529

Grailstone Press
P.O. Box 14285
St. Paul, MN 55114 USA

www.grailbooks.org

Christian Kabbalah

Contents

INTRODUCTION

The ideas and concerns of Christian Kabbalism sound quite strange to our modern ears. Within modern theology, and particularly in Protestant soil, there has sprung up a fundamental distrust of anything mystical. This distrust is directed even against any Christian mysticism that has originated in the Christian Church itself, seeing in it only the error of human effort to save itself. As it is, a number of dubious efforts have appeared today seeking to find an inner link between non-Christian mysticism and the Christian proclamation. If Christian theology is opposed above all to the mixing of Hindu or Buddhist mysticism with the Christian confession of faith, then connecting the Christian message with Jewish Kabbalistic mysticism appears as a mixing of religions that is especially off track. The rejection of mysticism in contemporary Protestant theology follows from a particular understanding of God's utter transcendence and of the absolute break that prevails in the relationship between God and man, an interpretation taken from the Old Testament idea of God.

Whether the view of mysticism prevailing today is right or wrong – I personally think it is wrong – we must nevertheless reckon with this attitude as a widespread prejudice. Such a hostile attitude, however, has not always held the field. In particular, the great surge of mysticism within the theology and theosophy of German pietism led not only to a renaissance in the study of the Kabbalah within Protestant theology, but also to a positive evaluation of the religious content of the Kabbalah in its own right.[1] No less than the leading head of the Christian theosophy of early Pietism, the Swabian prelate Friedrich Christoph Oetinger, developed a Christian Kabbalah not only in his writings, but also from his pulpit in Herrenberg. By no means was he alone in this regard. He was part of a specifically Swabian intellectual tradition, which harkened back to an earlier Swabian humanism, in particular to the great Hebraist, Reuchlin, who, at the risk of his life, argued against the governing body of the Dominican Inquisition in Cologne and the Holy See that the intellectual heirs of Judaism should be held in high esteem.

Moreover, a distinctive melding of Jewish-Kabbalistic and Christian mystical traditions was accomplished earlier in the older Protestant mysticism, particularly in the case of Jacob Boehme. His theosophy took up and assimilated many different Kabbalistic ideas, and a series of Kabbalistic notions and methods of exegesis are found in him once more – although this does not clarify the question of Jacob Boehme's Kabbalistic sources.[2] What is true for Jacob Boehme is true also for a large part of the Jacob Boehme school. By the 17th century, it had spread outside of Germany, throughout England and the Netherlands. It penetrated into the northern countries as far as Moscow. Particularly on Holland soil, and especially in Amsterdam, a connection between disciples of Jacob Boehme and Jewish Kabbalists was revived. In general, all theological circles influenced by Jacob Boehme – to which belonged such well-known natural scientists as Isaac Newton, Robert Fludd, and Francis Mercurius von Helmont – maintained a receptive openness to Kabbalistic ideas.

In regard to Christian Kabbalism, then, we are looking at an established intellectual current that could still maintain its place within churchly theology until ecclesiastical judgment against different mystical tendencies leading to certain radical spiritualistic phenomena brought about the expulsion of Pietism's radical sectarian elements. As a result, Christian Kabbalism was pushed out of the Church from the beginning of the Enlightenment, and since that time it has led a largely unknown life on the fringes of the Church, in the realm of theosophy and anthroposophy.

It seems to me that the present sensitivity on those points at which a Christian-Jewish encounter can begin anew requires once more a closer engagement with this neglected child of theology. For this project, Oetinger offers a most suitable point of departure. The Jewish Kabbalah played an important role in shaping his Christian theosophy, which he expounded as prelate of the Church established in Wurttemberg. What makes the study of this association particularly easy is the fact that Oetinger names his sources and authorities, so that we are not groping in the dark as we are with the older mystics and theosophists, whose Kabbalistic heirs, according to the most reliable authorities, can no longer be traced. Before we turn to Oetinger, however, we must make some remarks on the origins of Christian Kabbalism.

I.

THE BEGINNINGS OF CHRISTIAN KABBALISM

Christian Kabbalism is the interpretation of Kabbalistic themes in the context of the Christian faith, or an interpretation of Christian doctrines utilizing Kabbalistic methods and concepts. Its beginnings are generally traced back to Count Pico de la Mirandola, the well-known renaissance philosopher and creator of a Christian neo-Platonism.[3] When in 1486, at the age of twenty-three, Pico stepped into prominence with his 900 conclusions or theses on a Christian syncretism of all religions and sciences, he included the Jewish Kabbalah as the subject of a large number of those statements he intended to submit to Rome for general discussion. The basic idea he submitted to the humanists and theologians of his time was, in essence, nothing less than the thesis that esoteric Judaism is fundamentally identical with Christianity. Already, Pico de la Mirandola understood the Kabbalah as a proof vindicating his thesis that the heart of the Jewish religion, contrary to the assertions of Jewish Orthodoxy, shows an essential affinity with the Christian proclamation.

In his illuminating essay, *Zur Geschichte der Anfänge der christlichen Kabbala*,[4] [*On the History of the Beginning of the Christian Kabbalah*] Gershom Scholem, perhaps the most prominent expert on the history of Kabbalism, has drawn attention to the fact that Pico de la Mirandola was not the creator of a

Christian Kabbalism. Even before Pico, a Christian interpretation of the Kabbalah had been sought – by Jewish converts no less. It was one such Jewish convert who gave Pico de la Mirandola access to the Kabbalah: the Sicilian Jew, Samuel ben Nissim Abul Fradsch from Girgenti, who converted to Christianity. As a Christian and holder of lower priestly orders around 1467, he went by the name of Guglielmo Raimondo Moncada, and in the course of his rather quixotic life assumed even more names. The Latin translation of Kabbalistic writings, found in the Vatican Hebraic Codices 189-91, come from this convert. In these codices, he is named Flavius Mithridates. For several years, from 1485 on, he worked closely with Pico as his instructor in Hebrew and Chaldaean.[5]

Mithridates himself marks the end of a much older tradition of Jewish converts. The oldest witness for conversion to Christianity on the basis of Kabbalistic methods of exegesis that Scholem has found is Abraham Abulafia, who was born around 1240.[6] He seems to have in view a student prior to him, who studied with him in Capua, around 1280, and then fell into apostasy. Following a typical Kabbalistic method of letter-inversion, they had interpreted the phrase in the Song of Solomon: "I sat under the shade of my desire," (2.3) as, "His Cross I love," or, "In the shadow of his cross I love to dwell," or, "In the shadow of the Crucified One."

The first convert who refers explicitly to the Kabbalah is Abner von Burgos who, in his mature years, converted to Christianity around 1320 after a long inner struggle, and took the name Alfonso von Valladolid.[7] In lengthy explanations, and using the rabbinic interpretation of the Shekinah and the Jewish fragment on "The Measure of the Body" (of the Godhead) as a prototype, Alfonso sought to demonstrate the Christian doctrine of the Incarnation in Kabbalistic sources. Alfonso went so far as to identify the "Metatron" of the Kabbalah with the Person of the "Son" in the Christian doctrine of the Trinity who, in his Incarnation, was the "Sent One," an interpretation derived from an etymology of the word "Metatron" which was already widespread among Kabbalists of the 13th century.[8]

Earlier attempts such as these to interpret the Kabbalah in a Christian way led to the same reaction evoked by Christian Kabbalism over and again in later times. This reaction follows from the fact that orthodox teaching in both religions rejects the approximation of Kabbalistic doctrines to the Christian. Even Raymond Lull, the great champion for missions to the Muslims and Jews, who in his *Ars Magna* (Great Art), portrayed the Jewish Kabbalah as an embodiment of natural revelation that is completed in Christian revelation, was for that very reason rebuked by the Church for heresy.[9] Later, a papal commission would condemn Pico de la Mirandola because of his statement: "No science proves the divinity of Christ as well as Kabbalism and the *Magia*."[10]

Scholem also shows that Jewish Orthodoxy, too, vigorously resists the Christian interpretation of the Kabbalah in the same way. In the struggle that broke out in the 13th and 14th centuries over the Christian interpretation of the Kabbalah, one already finds most of the arguments that would be set forth in the 17th century by Orthodox Jews against Baron Knorr von Rosenroth's *The Kabbalah Unveiled*. For example, in a commentary on the *Schiur Komah*, written at the end of the 13th century, the attempt to find certain anaologies to the Christian doctrine of the Trinity in the Kabbalah is repudiated as an affront to Jewish doctrine.

In this polemic, one finds yet another opinion that maintains the Christian dogma of the Trinity and the Incarnation may have arisen from a deterioriation and misinterpretation of genuine Kabbalistic themes. In the writings of those who follow this opinion, Jesus and his disciples appear as real Kabbalists, "although their Kabbalah may have been full of mistakes." John and Paul in particular are considered as students of the Kabbalah who misinterpreted the Kabbalistic symbol of the Sefiroth and turned it into the doctrine of the Father, the Son (Logos) and Holy Spirit. In this manner, the Spanish professor, Profet Duran, in his anti-Christian work, *Schmach der Christen* [*The Shame of the Christians*], written in 1397, explains: "The doctrine of the Trinity, which they apply erroneously to the Godhead, in their case sprang from their going astray in this science (of the Kabbalah); namely, from the Kabbalistic idea of the three lights: the primal lights, the pure lights, and the radiant lights . . . just as their doctrine of the Incarnation may have originated from the 'Mystery of Investiture' (the Angels and souls in bodies), of which the Kabbalists speak."

In spite of these objections on the sides of Jewish and

Christian orthodoxy, Christian Kabbalism continued to develop in the 14th and 15th centuries. The fundamental doctrines of the Trinity and the Incarnation here, too, form the point of departure. The Christian doctrine of the Trinity is consistently linked with the Kabbalistic doctrine of the Sefiroth, the outflowings or emanations of the Godhead. In the 15th century, one can even find instances in which, by means of Christian Kabbalistic forgeries, a helping hand is given wherever genuine sources do not seem to prove clearly enough the desired connection between Kabbalistic and Christian teachings.[11] For example, in the work of a Spanish Maronite, Pedro de la Caballeria, under the title *Zeal of the Christian*, we find a typically Christian exegesis of the Trisagion drawn from Isaiah 6.3. It appears here as a quotation from the *Zohar*: "Holy – that is the Father; Holy – that is the Son; Holy – that is the Holy Spirit," intended to serve the mission among the Jews and Saracens.   This quotation was widely distributed. It is even to   be found on a marble slab in the Cathedral Court in Passau, which bears the inscription of Rabbi Simeon ben Jochai Filius, and so it goes back to the legendary author himself of the *Zohar*. This tradition can be traced further to Paulus de Heredia. He, too, was a Jewish convert. He was acquainted with Pico de la Mirandola and is described as his teacher. Through him, Pico also came into contact with the forgeries of the Kabbalistic pseudepigrapha, which come from a group of baptized Jews in Spain at the end of the 15th century. With the help of these forgeries, they proved "the Trinity, the Incarnation, the (Virgin) birth, the Glorification, and other dogmas on which they erected the pillars of their theses," as one orthodox Jewish polemicist wrote against these forgeries.[12]

This Christian Kabbalism of Jewish converts had, to be sure, little influence on the intellectual movements of the age. It made a deeper impression only when Pico took it up and raised it to a central theme of the Christian philosophy of the Renaissance. Through Pico, Christian Kabbalism penetrated to Germany, where Reuchlin became the founder of a distinctively Swabian branch of Christian Kabbalism, which can be traced from Princess Antonia to Oetinger.

Reuchlin was the first German scholar thoroughly to occupy himself with the Kabbalah.[13] The book of Gikatilla, *Schaare ora* [*Gates of Light*], in particular made a deep impression on him. This was a compendium of Kabbalistic philosophy that dealt with the doctrine of God, his names and outflowings (Sefiroth). Reuchlin had learned Hebrew with the imperial physician, the learned Jew Jacob ben Jehiel Loans, in Linz, in the years 1492 ff. In 1498, he was led into a deeper study of Hebrew language and literature by the learned Jew, Obadja Sforno. His Kabbalistic studies produced two books: *De Verbo Mirifico*, (*The Wonderworking Word*); and *De Arte Kabbalistica* (*On the Kabbalistic Art*). Both works represent the attempt to give a Christian interpretation of the Kabbalah. In both, the Jewish Kabbalah is recognized as an ur-revelation brought to mankind even before the birth of Christ, imparting insight into the sublime mysteries of the divine Being. Both works, however, show how these ur-revelations find their crown and fulfillment only in Christ.

In the book, *De Verbo Mirifico* (1494), a learned Jew, a Greek philosopher and Reuchlin himself carry on a conversation. They state that there is in the realm of spiritual matters a knowledge given only by divine revelation. God and man are joined by the "wondrous Word," through revelation of the mystery contained in the wondrous "Names" of God, and especially in the Tetragrammaton. These Names contain not only God's Being, but also the manner of his unfolding and radiance in the universe and in the history of salvation. However, even from Moses' Tetragrammaton there is a progressive development to the most wonderful of all Names: Jesus, through whom the inexpressible Name of God is first made expressible. To this Name of Jesus, in whom man and God are united, belongs all glory. This Name works wonders and redemption.

This book established Reuchlin's fame among his contemporaries. Agrippa von Nettesheim, who himself developed a Christian Kabbalism and traced the teaching of the Kabbalists on the Sefiroth to an interpretation of God's self-manifestation in creation in a book of his early years, *De occulta philosophia*, (*On Occult Philosophy*), was still holding readings on it in 1509.[14]

Reuchlin's *De Arte Kabbalistica* (1517) is also a dialogue. In the conversation between a Jew, a Muslim, and a Pythagorean, the Kabbalah appears as the perception of the higher world and its mysteries, revealed by an angel first to Adam, the first UrMan. It was then transmitted in an unbroken tradition to the men of the great Synagogue and finally to the

17

teachers of the Talmud. Concerning this Kabbalah, it is maintained that it may also be the source of Hellenistic philosophy, especially Pythagorean philosophy, which in its turn came into existence from Egyptian, Jewish and Persian Wisdom sources. It therefore describes those higher perceptions of the Kabbalah on the Being of God, on the Sefiroth, on form and perceptible things, the gate and path of knowledge, the angels and the heavenly spheres. Moreover, the different methods of Kabbalistic science – inversion of letters, treating the letters of a word as the first letters of other words (acronyms), exchanging letters; for example, the first with the last, the second with the next to last – are taught and illustrated with examples. This work, too, ends in a glorification of the Name of Jesus and of the Cross, which are explained using the above mentioned Kabbalistic technique of letter interpretation.

II.

OETINGER'S PATH TO THE KABBALAH

Already at twenty-three years of age, while he was studying in Tubingen, F.C. Oetinger was drawn to the rabbis. At the beginning of his theological studies, in 1721, he asserted that rabbinic study belonged with the fundamental sources of Christian theology.[15] "Let me announce the two resources I used *ab ovo* (from the beginning) to study theology. These were the rabbis and philosophy, since they both draw from Holy Scripture. When I compare the style of Ecclesiastes with the style of Proverbs, methinks I am listening to something with a rabbinic taste. . . In order to enter this most ancient way of thinking, valued so differently by us, I read the rabbis for a year and a day, sometimes with the reader Bernhard, sometimes alone. I disciplined myself to do this because I was possessed of a great desire to think like an ancient Jew. Of course, if one hasn't disciplined oneself as a boy, it's too late when one gets older." He names the rabbinic authors whom he studied: Rabbi Joseph Albo (*Sepher Ikarim*), Rabbi Saadia (*Sepher Amunah*), Rabbi Abarbanel (*Maschmiah Jeschuah*), Rabbi Michael Jophi, Rabbi Bechai, then continues. "Nevertheless, I found that the rabbis no longer write purely after the style of Rabbi Simeon ben Jochai in the *Zohar*. Therefore, I sought opportunity to read the Kabbalistic sources themselves. But because it is difficult, I sought opportunity to associate with learned and experienced Jews."

From the beginning, then, Oetinger's study of books stands next to his personal association with scholars of the Jewish tradition. And, from the beginning, next to his study of the rabbis stands his study of the *Zohar* itself, as his reference to the *Zohar* shows. Gaon Saadia is the best-known representative of German Hasidism.[16] Isaac Abarbanel (1437 – 1508) is the father of the well-known Leone Ebreo, whose *Dialoghi d'Amore* (Dialogues of Love) links the Kabbalistic tradition with Platonism and neo-Platonism.[17] Simeon ben Jochai, whom Oetinger credits as the author of the *Zohar*, takes us to the heart of the Kabbalistic tradition itself.[18]

Already during his time of study, Oetinger carried on a learned correspondence with a circle in Frankfurt which studied the Kabbalah. This circle had been formed when Spener founded his "Collegia pietatis" in Frankfurt, a circle whose separatist, anti-Church tendencies had quite irritated him. The lawyer, Johann Jakob Schütz, at that time had taken sides with the most extreme and zealous members of this early pietistic conventical in Frankfurt, and was a fanatical follower of Eleonore von Merlau, who was later the spouse of the chiliast, J.W.Petersen, also highly esteemed by Schütz. In this radically awakened circle of early pietism, Knorr von Rosenroth's *Kabbalah Unveiled* was especially admired. The councilor, Fende, and the unmarried daughter of Johann Jacob Schütz continued the intellectual legacy of the genial lawyer with missionary zeal. Fende published various writings in which he set forth a Christian interpretation of Kabbalistic doctrines, which he came across in Knorr von Rosenroth's *Kabbalah Unveiled*. However, his Christian doctrine was not entirely orthodox. The doctrine of the Trinity and

Christology that he discovered in the Kabbalah to him appeared to justify the Trinitarian doctrine and Christology of Arius rather than that of Athanasius. This is quite correct, actually, insofar as the original Jewish doctrine of the "Wisdom of God" and other divine hypostases, such as the "Shekinah" are seen in these hypostases not as elements of the divine Being, but as creatures of God. Thus, in the oldest Jewish doctrine of Wisdom, Wisdom is the first of God's creatures.[19] Among creatures, she of course occupies the highest rank, of all creatures standing nearest to God. But she never appears as God himself or as of the same being-essence as God. In point of fact, she therefore occupies the same place as the Logos in the theology of Arius, who also is described as the first of all creatures, who stands nearest to God, but who is not of the same being-essence as God.

During this time of his study, Oetinger learned the Kabbalah only in this interpretation of Fende's, which saw it as the principal witness for justifying Arian Christology and doctrine of God, and he felt his orthodoxy greatly shaken. He wrote about this in his autobiography: "At the same time [during his study in Tübingen, which he finished in 1725], we read the different booklets of the councilor, Fende. In these booklets, he set forth the teachings of the well-known lawyer, Schütz, as his favorite disciple, and from the *Kabbalah Unveiled* he wanted to clothe the statements of Arius with expressions from the New Testament. This created in us such anguish of soul that we decided we would make a thorough study, especially of all those passages in Holy Scripture that deal with the

21

divinity of Christ or of the form of God in Christ."[20]

Later, after thoroughly studying the Kabbalah, Oetinger would always maintain that the Sefiroth are not creatures but forms of the manifestation of God, the forms of his expression and emanations of the divine Being within the world of creatures. However, he was never rid of the fear that the Kabbalistic doctrine of the Sefiroth, particularly the doctrine of the *Adam Kadmon*, could be misunderstood in an Arian sense and so undo his own effort at an orthodox interpretation of the doctrine of the Sefiroth in the sense of the Church's doctrine of the Trinity. Even in his chief dogmatic work, *Theologia ex idea vitae deducta* (*Theology Drawn from the Idea of Life*), published in the year 1765, a writing which rooted the whole theology of nature and history in the notion of a continuous unfolding and manifestation of the ineffable Divine life, he recalls how the councilor, Fende, in his explanation of the *Kabbalah Unveiled*, drew his Arian interpretation of the Kabbalah from the work of Rabbi Luria, which was stamped in the same mold. There, Oetinger argued against Rabbi Luria's supposed identification of the *Adam Kadmon* with the Logos, whom Luria understood as the Ab-Image of God, an Outframing or Conception; Oetinger saw in this concept the root of later Arian Christology.[21]

Now a visit to Frankfurt will bring Oetinger, thirsty for knowledge, into immediate contact with the actual Kabbalistic sources of his hitherto literary friends.

III.

22

KNORR VON ROSENROTH

The long awaited opportunity to meet learned experts on the Kabbalah in person came to Oetinger in the year 1729 on his first journey, which led him to Frankfurt. In a strange coincidence, he encountered Christian and Jewish Kabbalism in the same house. He stayed with the same councilor, Fende, with whom he had already kept up a scholarly correspondence on Patristic questions. In Fende's house, he met the young lady Schütz, the very learned daughter of the well-known lawyer-solicitor, Johann Jacob Schütz (1640-1690).[22] She gave to Oetinger Baron Knorr von Rosenroth's *The Kabbalah Unveiled*. Most of us know Johann Jacob Schütz and Knorr von Rosenroth today only from the hymnal. Schütz is the composer of the hymn, "Praise and Honor Be to the Most High God;" and Rosenroth composed the hymn, "Morning Glory of Eternity, Light of the Uncreated Light." Only very few who sing this hymn have any idea that the whole Kabbalistic tradition of the Shekinah – the "Glory" of God – and of the Sefiroth have found their spontaneous, artistic expression in this hymn – interpreted, to be sure, in a Christian way.

Knorr von Rosenroth (1639-1689) had come to know the Kabbalah in two ways.[23] Early in his youth, he had applied himself assiduously to Hebraic Studies. Later, during a study trip from 1663-1666, which led him to Holland, France and England, he came into contact with Kabbalistic Jewish circles for the first time in Holland, more precisely in Amsterdam, where Thomas di Pinedo and Isaac di Rocamora were living at the time. It is certain that while he was there, he pursued intense Kabbalistic studies with Rabbi Meir Stern, head of the synagogue of the German Jews from Frankfurt am Main. His zeal for the Kabbalah was not at all out of step with the missionary interests of that time, which were zealously cultivated in the Christian pietistic conventicles – "Winkeln" as they were called in Holland – of that time.

In England he became acquainted with a form of Christian Kabbalism that, for its part, stood in intellectual connection with the Kabbalistic Christian neo-Platonism of the Italian renaissance, especially with the tradition of Pico de la Mirandola. In England, he came upon the two greatest Christian Kabbalists of the time. The one had been the head of the Platonizing school of Cambridge, Henry More (1614-1687),[24] and the other was More's friend, Franciscus Mercurius van Helmont (1618-1699), son of the great Dutch physician, Baptista van Helmont. These introduced Knorr von Rosenroth to a system of religious philosophy that linked the Jewish Kabbalah, neo-Platonic philosophy, modern science and, not least, a rich portion of Jacob Boehme's theosophy in the closest possible connection. In Henry More and Van Helmont, Knorr von Rosenroth found expressed the two main ideas that brought him to a more intensive engagement of the Kabbalah. One was the idea that the Kabbalah represents a form of primal revelation that, from the beginning of the world, has accompanied humanity's spiritual development in the form of an esoteric, mystical knowledge. The other was the idea that the Jewish and Christian faiths in their esoteric kernels are identical to one another. In other words, the Jewish Kabbalah already contains the truths of the Christian faith, and leads to them.

Knorr von Rosenroth's work, published under the title, *Cabbala Denudata* [*The Kabbalah Unveiled*], is essentially a commentary on the *Zohar*,[25] the most important writing of the Jewish Kabbalah. For centuries, it enjoyed a canonical standing next to the Old Testament and the Talmud. According to the Talmudic tradition, the *Zohar* goes back to Rabbi Simeon ben Jochai, who died in the 2nd century several years after the destruction of Jerusalem. Knorr von Rosenroth held to this authorship of the book as firmly as did the other representatives of the Christian Kabbalah of his time: Henry More and Franciscus Mercurius van Helmont. This explains the frequently repeated assertions of these authors, viz., that with respect to the author of the *Zohar*, we are dealing with a contemporary of the apostle Paul.

The Talmudic tradition also gives an unusual biographical foundation for the inspired, visionary character of the *Zohar*. According to this tradition, Rabbi Simeon ben Jochai was banned by another Rabbi in cahoots with the Roman authorities on account of derogatory remarks made concerning cultural works of the Romans. Fearing persecution, Simeon ben Jochai hid with his son in a cave, where they buried themselves up to their necks in the sand and spent the entire day studying the Law. Wondrously, there sprang up in the cave a carob-bean tree, and a water fountain that kept them alive. There in the cave a spiritual knowledge of the way to enlightenment

25

was imparted to them in twelve yearly meditations. These were later set down in writing in the book of the *Zohar*. After twelve years, the prophet Elijah came and placed himself in the entrance of the cave, and cried out: "Who will tell the son of Jochai that Caesar is dead and that the ban is lifted?" Then, "they went out and saw how men were plowing and sowing."

As new research has established, the book of the *Zohar* reaches back to older Kabbalistic traditions. However, in its present form, it is the work of a later author, presumably the Kabbalist Moses de Leon, who lived in Guadalajara, a city in Castille, then led a life of wandering and finally died after a momentary stay in Avila, in the year 1305 on his return journey from Valladolid to Avila in Arevalo. The first volume by Knorr von Rosenroth gives a Latin commentary to the text of the book of the *Zohar*, which contains a large part of the later Kabbalistic tradition of the Jews.

The content of *The Kabbalah Unveiled* perhaps is most vividly expressed on its title page. There, one sees the figure of a woman, her mantel sliding from an already bare shoulder. She steps up to the gate of a palace that bears the inscription: "Palace of Mystery." The wing of the gate is already open with the help of a key, which the woman holds on a strap hanging over her left arm. The woman's face is turned upward; her eyes gaze on a vision of divine Light, a sun encircled by a wreath of sunbeams, which shine out of a dark cloud. In the sunshine appear three circles of light, which altogether enclose ten circles of light. The first light contains three, the second seven, the third one. This represents the ten Sefiroth or mirrored-splendors in which the divine Light comprehends itself. In her right hand, the woman holds a burning candle. In her left, a scroll that contains on the inside the Old Testament, with the first words of Genesis (in Hebrew): "in the Beginning, God created [heaven and earth]." On the outside, it contains the New Testament with the first words of John's Gospel (in Greek): "In the Beginning was the Word." With her right foot, she steps on the wave of a storm-tossed sea, a ship pushing on in the distance. With her left foot, she stands on the edge of a cave in which the chemical signs of minerals appear. An inscription explains the meaning of the individual gestures. On the cylinder of the two Testaments is: Eplicat (She explains). Over her eyes, it reads: Alta videt (She sees the cave). On the candle is: Lucet (She illumines). Under her right foot: Dominat (She masters [passion]). Under her left foot: Alterat (She transforms metals). And, on the threshold: Intrat (She enters). The inscriptions are explained further in the following epigram (in Latin):

She illumines the ambiguous passages of the Old and New Testaments.
She beholds the Exalted One and makes known the Trinity in its ten names.
Illumined in spiritual light, She disperses the pagan darkness.
She masters the inner whirlpool, which incites passion.
She disentangles the tangled veins of bronze in the heart.
She enters the inner sanctum and illumines its concealed chambers.[26]

The Kabbalah here is decisively set forth in the

form of Wisdom. She unlocks the Old as well as the New Testaments. She possesses the "intelligentia spiritualis" (spiritual understanding) of the mystery of the Old and New Covenants. Primarily, the Kabbalah makes the entire Holy Scriptures, the obscure passages of both Testaments, accessible to spiritual understanding.

The statement concerning the vision of God is also revealing. She makes known the Trinity under its tenfold names, which are called under the names of the ten Sefiroth, the divine Ur-Light reflected in its ten splendors. The Christian doctrine of the Trinity is contained in the Kabbalistic doctrine of the ten outgoings or mirrored-splendors of Divinity.

The basic purpose, therefore, is to present a Christian Kabbalah. Indeed, Knorr von Rosenroth saw in the Kabbalah not only the point of the inner conjunction between Judaism and Christianity, but what is more, he ascribes an ecumenical mission to it. In the introductory letter of his treatise, *Über den Nutzen einer Übersetzung des kabbalistischen Buches Sohar* [*On the Need for a Translation of the Kabbalistic Book of the Zohar*],[27] he writes: The many divisions among the Christian religions had no other cause than the differences of philosophical principles and metaphysical definitions, which form the so-called left hand of theology, which prevail among the Christians themselves. These divisions founded on the differences of philosophical presuppositions could at best be overcome by resorting to the oldest philosophy that was in vogue in the time of Christ and the apostles themselves, and which sprang out of the Holy Scriptures as from a common source. The Kabbalah here appears as that form of philosophy which makes it possible to overcome the strife of later theological schools and confessions by ascertaining the primordial meaning of the divine revelation or manifestation.

On the other hand, Knorr von Rosenroth did not conceal the fact that the ultimate aim of his Christian Kabbalism was missionary in nature. So he writes in answer to a letter of Henry More, reproduced in its original English version, dated 22 April 1675.[28] "I extend my highest commendation to your zealous effort to convert the Jews. Truly, this is the worthy endeavor of a man who is Christian not just in name but also in fact. I also approve of your thesis that to begin such an undertaking, it is not only useful but also essential that Christians and Jews study each other's theology or theosophy. Any contribution to such a mutual understanding is not to be undervalued by anyone who would serve as an interpreter of both sides. Therefore, not only the republic of scholars, but the whole of Christendom owes you the profoundest gratitude, because you have taken yourself into this difficult field."

Aside from his missionary aim, however, Knorr von Rosenroth saw the primary importance of an exegesis of the Kabbalah lying in the common endeavor of Jewish and Christian scholars to ascertain the basis of theology in an objective investigation of truth.[29] For the same reason, Knorr von Rosenroth pointed out in the introduction of his reflection upon the need for a translation of the *Zohar* that such a translation brings about not only a deeper knowledge of Jewish theology, but it also leads to a better understanding of many passages in the New Testament.[30] This applies not only to understanding Jewish forms of literal expression in the New Testament or in Jewish antiquities, to which it refers, but also to the understanding of its inner sense.[31]

The second volume of *The Kabbalah Unveiled* includes, in its first and second parts, a Latin translation of several important books of the *Zohar* itself; namely, the *Siphra di Zeniutha* (*Book of Mysteries*), the *Idra Rabba* (*Great Synod*), and the *Idra Suta* (*Lesser Synod*), and commentaries on these books by Rabbi Isaac Luria and Rabbi Naphtali Hirtz. There is found first and foremost a systematic summary of the doctrines of the book of the *Zohar* (*Synopsis dogmatum vulgatiorum totius libri Sohar*). Also in this second volume, the fundamental tendency of a Christian interpretation is expressed when the author appends in each case passages of the New Testament that parallel the systematic introduction of the presentation of the particular doctrines of the Kabbalistic system, in order to establish in this manner how the Kabbalistic and New Testament traditions are inwardly connected.[32]

The third part of the *Kabbalah Unveiled* bears the title *Pneumatica Kabbalistica* (*The Kabbalistic Doctrine of the Spirit*). It contains sections on the Kabbalistic doctrine of the Spirit, on the good and bad angels, and on the soul and its different stations and transformations (specifically, the Kabbalistic doctrine of the transmigration of souls). It sets the Latin translation of the tractate *Beth Elohim* (House of the

Lord) by Rabbi Abraham Cohen Irira from Portugal alongside the tractate *De revolutionibus animarum* (*On the revolution of the soul*), which stems from the school of Rabbi Luria and was translated into Latin by the Christian Kabbalist, Franciscus Mercurius van Helmont, in which the same van Helmont summarizes his Kabbalistic studies, and sets up a systematic connection of Kabbalistic and Christian doctrines. In the title of this writing by van Helmont, *Synopsis of the Christian Kabbalah*, the notion of the "Christian Kabbalah" steps to the front: "*Adumbratio Kabbalae Christianae, idest Syncatabasis Hebraizans, sive Brevis Applicatio Doctrinae Hebraeorum Kabbalisticae ad Dogmata novi foederis; pro formanda Hypothesi, ad Conversionem Judaeorum proficua*" (*A sketch of Christian Kabbalism, i.e. a Hebraic conceptualization, or a brief application of the Hebraic Kabbalistic doctrines to the dogmas of the New Covenant; in order to form an hypothesis useful for converting the Jews.*)[33]

This sketch is a dialogue between a Kabbalistic and Christian philosopher, in which both are concerned at first simply to instruct the other on each one's particular doctrines of belief, and then they ascertain, to their own surprise, a profound agreement of Kabbalistic and Christian doctrines of faith. Ostensibly, this tractate is significant for the history of Jewish-Christian relations because the Christian philosopher cites New Testament passages, which he brings forward in order to establish his doctrines in Hebraic form. Van Helmont, therefore, used a Hebrew translation of the New Testament, and characteristically, it is precisely the notions and images of the Hebraic New Testament that reveal the amazing agreement of the Kabbalistic and Christian traditions.

The very fact that Knorr von Rosenroth placed this system of a Christian Kabbalah, presented in the form of a religious conversation between a Christian philosopher and a Jewish Kabbalist, at the conclusion of his *Kabbalah Unveiled* throws into clear relief the basic intention of his work.

From Knorr von Rosenroth's *Kabbalah Unveiled*, a powerful stream of Kabbalistic ideas flows through the intellectual life of Europe. Among his admirers, there is found, next to the leaders of German pietism such as Spener and August Hermann Francke, and scholars such as J. Christian Wagensil and the Orientalist Hermann von der Hardt from Helmstadt, none less than Leibniz, who in 1687 stopped in Sulzbach for 10 days and kept up a detailed conversation with the well-known Knorr von Rosenroth on the *Kabbalah Unveiled*. In Sulzbach, he also was shown the still unfinished manuscript of a further work by Rosenroth, the *Messias puer*, (*The Messiah Child*) and was so taken by it that he spoke of it frequently in his letters and writings. In them, he regularly expresses unrestrained praise of Knorr von Rosenroth, praising him as he did none other of his contemporaries.[34]

Leibniz also stressed how Knorr von Rosenroth may have illumined in his work the inner points of contact and continuity between Jewish and Christian theology from the Kabbalah, contrary to the interests of the representatives of dogmatic orthodoxy of both religions. Thus, he writes in a letter to the Count,

Ernst von Hessen-Rheinfels, to whom he reported his meeting with Knorr von Rosenroth: "There are found some excellent things concerning the Messiah, which modern Jews ignore or seek to suppress, or to distort their true sense."[35] In another letter to the Count, he emphasizes the immediate, inner connection of the Kabbalah with Christian truth,[36] "Witnesses are foreshadowed in the Kabbalistic writings of the Jews as he (Knorr von Rosenroth) observes. He showed to me his own work in progress entitled, *Messias puer*, in which he admirably illustrates the history of Christ from the Annunciation to his baptism, drawn from the Gospels, among other sources, then from passages of the ancient Kabbalists."

From this never completed work, *Messias puer*, Lebniz looked for a definitive explanation on the life and preaching of Jesus. "Shortly, we will become free from these scruples, when the *Messias puer* of Mr. Knorr comes to the light of day and he explains to us the history of Christ, as it is described by the Gospels, from rabbinic and Kabbalistic writings . . . We look for what Mr. Knorr will teach on this point."[37]

Subsequently, he drew attention to this work so much in his *Monthly Conversations of Some Good Friends*, (1689, p. 1265) that it must have been all the more difficult for him in the following year (1690, p. 1145) to disappoint the expectations he had raised among his learned friends by the news: "One deeply regrets that the Lord Chancellor Knorr died in Sulzbach and therefore the scholarly world is deprived not only of his *Messias puer* but also other rare writings."[38] In the estate of Leibniz, one finds still a series of letters in which Leibniz along with Franciscus Mercurius van Helmont has in mind the publication of this legacy of Knorr von Rosenroth, which van Helmont had in view, but it was never realized.

This *Kabbalah Unveiled* now comes to meet Oetinger in Frankfurt, in the house of Fende.

IV.

KOPPEL HECHT

In the house of councilor Fende, Oetinger also made the acquaintance of the well-known Kabbalist from the Jewish community in Frankfurt, Koppel Hecht. He represented a Kabbalism which, as had been done by Leone Ebreo, effected a synopsis of Jewish and Platonic mysticism. Oetinger wrote of his meeting with him in Frankfurt:

This man quite endeared himself to me on account of the unusual question of Jewish philosophy: viz., what were the 'broad face' and the 'small face' in God? Thereupon, I came to him right at the time of the Feast of Tabernacles. He demonstrated to me from the most rare documents, from chronology and from the Talmud that Plato had been a disciple of Jeremiah, and got his fundamental ideas from him. I thank God for this dispensation. For quite some time I had wondered where Plato got his description of the City of God that agrees so well with the Apocalypse. I could not understand how he came to write so emphatically of the Word from the beginning, and of the three most high Sefiroth or the three forms of divinity, or where he obtained his doctrine of the eternal Ideas or of the Original-Urimages of creatures in God, since he writes that physics must be grounded in experiment, theology in the declarations of God; or why Plato so often refers to the centrality of knowledge, when he says: 'I know that I am a member of the higher world and have acquired eternal life with an indescribable Light. However, since I have sunk in my frailty from contemplation of that pure knowledge into imagination, that Light has left me.'"[39]

Four years later, in the introduction to his *Public Memorial of the Teaching Tablet of Princess Antonia*, p. 18, on the mystery of the Three and the Seven in

God (this refers to his Kabbalistic interpretation of the Christian doctrine of the Trinity), it reads: "Faith has a great firmness and power, even though there are large gaps of understanding in it. This much I learned from the chronological reckoning of the Jew, Koppel Hecht: Plato heard only a little from the Babylonian wise men, Jeremiah and Ezekiel. He himself did not understand it."[40] Accordingly, he took the Kabbalistic doctrine of the Sefiroth as an occasion to critize the ecclesiastical doctrine of the Trinity. He explained, for example, that the Second Person of the Church's Trinity may in reality be the Shekinah (Glory) become man, while the doctrine of the Third Person of the Holy Spirit may go back to a false interpretation of the Jewish doctrine of Hochmah (Wisdom). Such thoughts may even have caused Koppel Hecht to describe Oetinger as "strange" on account of his Christian doctrines, and may have brought Oetinger himself to avoid using the term "persons" in his doctrine of the Trinity, in order not to give rise to the impression of tritheism.

It is even more significant, however, that Koppel Hecht himself already had crossed the road to Christian Kabbalism. Not only did he give Oetinger to know that he believed the Messiah may indeed have come, but for his part, referred him to Jacob Boehme as the prophet of a Kabbalism more clear than what existed in the book of the *Zohar*:

I cherished him (Koppel Hecht) all the more, and wondered how I should set about to understand the Kabbalah. He said that I should save myself the trouble and not bother with it. I should remain with the text of Holy Scripture. As far as the Kabbalah is concerned, we Christians have a book that speaks even more clearly than the Kabbalah. I asked, which book is that? He answered: Jacob Boehme. Then he declared to me that Boehme and the Kabbalists spoke in the same way. So that I wondered even more if he were not a Christian. Finally, he showed me the Syrian New Testament, which he always reads, and said, the Messiah may indeed have come. But, he could not take himself to the Christians because they have such strange doctrines. Our explanation of the Trinity is quite contrary to reason. He said there could be no separation of persons in God. The Messiah could not be viewed as the Second Person. The proof may be in the King Messiah. This figure may in the *Zohar* be higher than the created world, but in the Kabbalistic sense he is always explained as the King Messiah, not as the Second Person. It must be explained in an entirely different way if it is to satisfy conscience.

This remark characterizes a definite attitude of Christian Kabbalism, which we find again later in Oetinger's explanation of the Kabbalist doctrines. While the Kabbalah can support the idea that the Kabbalistic prophecies concerning the Messiah have been fulfilled in Jesus Christ, they cannot be made to accept the dogmatic formulations of the Church's doctrine of the Trinity in those passages where they set up a different exposition of the inner-divine Life in the sense of the Kabbalistic doctrine of the Sefiroth. Thus, the Christian Kabbalists may draw near to Christianity from Judaism, but they will never find the full approval of ecclesiastical dogma. By the same token, the Christian Kabbalists who come from Christianity, for their part fall very easily into conflict with their received Church teaching and also not infrequently with their Church authorities. The esoteric group of

Jews and Christians, therefore, are pushing the limits of their respective religions.

When the inhabitants of this border region discover that they are drawing near to brothers standing on the other side of the border, perplexing conversions on both sides often follow. There are not only Jews who, under the influence of the Kabbalah, consummate the move to Christianity by an actual act of conversion to the Christian Church; there are also Christians who, under the influence of the Kabbalah, convert to Judaism. Thus, a disciple of Jacob Boehme, Johann Peter Spaeth, impressed by the astonishing agreement of Jacob Boehme's teaching with the Jewish Kabbalah, converted to Judaism at the end of the 17th century and provoked a powerful reaction among Jews and Christians.[41] Joachim Schoeps, who draws from new sources to give a detailed appraisal of Johann Peter Spaeth in his work *Philosemitism in Baroque* (Tubingen, 1952), denies that Johann Peter Spaeth, alias Moses Germaus, was really a Kabbalist. Nevertheless, his investigations confirm that Spaeth's acquaintance with Christian Kabbalists initiated his conversion to Judaism. Thus, Spaeth worked with Knorr von Rosenroth in the composition of his *Kabbalah Unveiled*,[42] and for a long time stood under the influence of the writings of Franciscus Mercurius van Helmont, who was also among the adepts of Christian Kabbalism.

When, in his later conversion, Spaeth explicitly dissociated himself from Van Helmont's Kabbalistic teachings as well as those of Knorr von Rosenroth, and even from Jacob Boehme, and when he even recommended that Knorr von Rosenroth's translation of the *Zohar* be burned, this does not speak against his knowledge of the Kabbalah, but rather for his feeling after his conversion to Judaism that the Christian interpretation of the Kabbalah and its dispersion through publications was a profanation of the Kabbalah itself. Thus, he justified his call to burn Knorr von Rosenroth's translation of the *Zohar* on the grounds that it imparted difficult esoteric things "to the wild rabble and the unworthy," and in this way prostituted these esoteric things. When he diligently maintains, in reference to his literary opponents, that, "I sincerely confess that I do not understand the Kabbalah, yet this much I know: they understand it even less who think they understand it," this is no evidence that he did not understand the Kabbalah but an indication that he saw himself as an initiate who, as such, knew sufficiently well that he had not attained to the highest level of knowledge, but who nevertheless felt justified in describing his opponents as outsiders and dilettantes in the Kabbalah.[43]

. In this connection, Spaeth deserves special notice not only because he personally converted from Christianity to Judaism as a result of the Kabbalah, but also because he believed this to be the only way to effect a reconciliation between Judaism and Christianity. He called out to the Christians so deeply upset over his conversion: "Non vos deserui, sed praecessi (I am not running away from you; rather, I am going on ahead of you)." He basically saw his step as a prophetic and paradigmatic act, a model for the encounter between Judaism and Christianity.

But let us return to Oetinger. Not only had the communication with Koppel Hecht stamped for the time being his understanding of Plato; Oetinger also repeatedly made it well known in his later theosophical writings that the Kabbalist from Frankfurt was the one who imparted to him this knowledge. Thus, he reports three decades later in his writing on *The Golden Age* of 1759, concerning the eschatological outlook of Platonic philosophy (p. 4): "Whoever reads Plato diligently, will find at the end of the *Phaedo*, the *Gorgias*, and also the ninth book of the *Laws* many excellent things on the creation of the earth. The heathen desired accounts of the future world, as did the Christians. According to the book of *Patricius*, from a collegium he held with Aristotle, Plato reports that he heard similar accounts of the Babylonian philosophers; and, when I was in Frankfurt, I very much enjoyed my time with a learned Jew, Koppel Hecht by name, when he proved to me in great detail that Plato was a disciple of Jeremiah." In the supplement to the Plato passages from the *Golden Age*, he adds a list of complete Old Testament passages – there are over seventy – which are set forth by Abarbanel "in his splendid book, *Maschmiah Jeschuah*, or the Herald of Salvation, or of the Evangel" of the future *Golden Age*. His own biblical grounding for the doctrine of the *Golden Age*, which is his own eschatology, is thoroughly shaped by the Kabbalistic exegesis of the Old Testament in Abarbanel.

It is not without a certain charm to note that in Frankfurt not only did the Jewish and Christian Kabbalists make an impression on Oetinger, but also the lady who played the role of arbiter. The Christian Kabbalah stepped forth to meet him in the form of the young lady Schütz, daughter of the well-known professor of jurisprudence, Schütz. Of her, he wrote:

No sooner had I entered (the house of the councilor Fende), when the well-endowed maiden, little Schutzie, came down to meet me from the upper room of the Schütz's house. Under her arm she carried Baron Rosenroth's *Kabbalah Unveiled* and she offered it to me. She also offered me some money, and through Fende gave me to understand that it would be good if I stayed in Frankfurt and studied there. In the midst of such great wealth, she disdained the idea of herself getting married. She preferred contemplation and was an intelligent conversationalist, since her lord father, the well-known lawyer, had instructed her in her youth in all kinds of sciences and in the Holy Scriptures. However, on one occasion, when I began to show myself too grateful for her demonstrations of kindness, she became indifferent and chided me somewhat for my affected civility; it did not suit her seriousness. I wanted nothing, for I was quite satisfied with the *Kabbalah Unveiled*, since this book is difficult to obtain.[44]

While the book in this instance outshone its giver, the matter appears a bit different with the Jewish Kabbalah. After Oetinger recounted the above-mentioned conversation with Koppel Hecht concerning Plato's dependence on Jeremiah, he continued: "Once, while he was speaking to me of Plato, he used the phrase, such beautiful historical records. I gave him a rather quizzical look. His young daughter was sitting by my side. At that moment, she looked at me, and I looked at her, my gaze lingering on her for just a bit, so that he chided me: did I not know the saying from Job 31.1: 'I have made a covenant with my eyes. Why should I think upon a maid?' I apologized, saying that I was regarding her mind, not her flesh; but it did not help. I was, of course, in the wrong. But I took it to heart. It has often occurred to me that even though it was an awkward moment, it was still a good lesson from him."[45]

V.

ISAAC LURIA

Koppel Hecht led Oetinger only a few steps further into the Kabbalah, and otherwise referred him to Boehme. However, he could not keep the neophyte from longing after a deeper initiation into the mysteries of the Kabbalah. This he got from another teacher, a Kabbalist whom he met in Halle in the same year, but whose name he unfortunately withholds from us. Nonetheless, we know that he took another important step there. The unnamed Kabbalistic Jew in Halle initiated him in the teaching of the greatest Kabbalist of German Jewry, Isaac Luria. He inspired in Oetinger such enthusiasm for Luria, that Oetinger paid a goodly sum to purchase from him a manuscript of the most important work on Luria, *Ez Chaim* (*Tree of Life*) and gave "all my thanks for the philosophiam sacram Kabbalisticam (sacred Kabbalistic philosopher)."[46]

Luria's thought had the greatest influence on Oetinger. Unfortunately, no one has yet pursued the task of investigating carefully this influence. In all his later theological, theosophical as well as homiletical works, Oetinger repeatedly refers to Luria, whom he counted next to Jacob Boehme and Swedenborg as principal witnesses of spiritual knowledge. The many quotations from Luria found in Oetinger show that he considered Luria as an important proof for the idea that Kabbalistic theology itself points to its fulfillment in the Christian revelation. Therefore, Oetinger quite spontaneously set out on the same path taken by the first Christian Kabbalists, the path of using the Kabbalah for the apologetic and missionary purpose of leading orthodox Jews to the truth of the Christian faith by demonstrating that the truth of Christian faith is contained already in the esoteric tradition of the Jew's own religion.

Perhaps the most significant statement Oetinger made about Luria is found in his *Gedanken zur*

Vertheidigung J.Boehmes [*Thoughts on the Defense of Jacob Boehme*].[47] This work was composed during Oetinger's first journey, when Koppel Hecht referred him to the affinity between the Kabbalah and Jacob Boehme, and the Jew from Halle referred him to Luria. It showed that the young theologian had the courage of his convictions, because he defends both Jacob Boehme, who was condemned by the Church as a heretic, and the Jewish Kabbalist, Luria, and he links them directly together. To that extent, the report about Luria carries historical significance; for the first time, it conveys to German Pietism its connection with Hasidism, with which in so many respects it is closely related spiritually. He writes:

Let us also note this among the memorable events in the revelation of Christ's Kingdom. Shortly before the birth of Jacob Boehme – a man on whom the Spirit of Elijah was poured out and who was abundantly crowned by the heavenly Shekina or Sophia – there lived in Jerusalem a man by the name of Isaac Luria. His career is described in the Kabbalistic book *Emek Hamelek* (Valley of Kings), and deserves a special treatise. Of this godly man, J. Boehme surely knew nothing. Even so, his teachings agree remarkably with Luria's, except that the latter, speaking in Hebrew, pursued incomparably higher the mystery of the meanings of characters, signatures and words, which was all the more necessary for persuading the Jews who seek after signs. Therefore, whoever among the Jews wanted to be called a "Hasid," i.e. a righteous or a good man (Rom 5.7), would rise up every midnight upon this man's written council and pray for the imminent appearing of Moses and Elijah (of which we have confirmation in the *Apocalypse*, chptr 11), and redemption from their final captivity. Of this, I have a specific example in a report of a godly Jew in Italy. To him personally, Moses and Elijah used to come around midnight, as on Mt. Tabor, and they would speak with him of the restoration of the fallen house of David that was drawing near.

To return to Isaac Luria. His book, called *The Tree of Life*, is an explanation received from above of the very obscure book called *Zohar*, which existed and indeed was even well known in Paul's time. Its author was a man who sat in a cave for 12 years. Simeon son of Jochai was his name. Isaac Luria was accustomed to practice his devotions at his grave every year of his life. For love of him, permission was granted angels and spirits of the higher school to reveal knowledge of the future world, yet in a cryptic style of writing, until the last generation of the kingly Messiah should come, since all children should know and understand this highest knowledge. One cannot deny the splendor that comes to light in the letters of these excellent men among the Israelites.

Because the Kabbalah of the Jews, when compared to the dominant light of the Spirit that proceeds from Jesus Christ, is a transfiguring light that barely shines, so to speak, these men form a contrasting backdrop against which the force of the saying in II Cor 3.17-18 shines forth with an even greater majesty than before: 'Now the Lord is the Spirit, and where the Spirit of the Lord is, there is liberty. But we all, with unveiled face, beholding as in a glass the glory of the Lord, are changed into the same image from glory to glory, even as by the Spirit of the Lord.'

According to the hidden dispensation of God, it was

not yet revealed to this Isaac Luria that the Name of Jesus is the 'name above all names,' because he was an Israelite. Even so, as the book he wrote, *Noph Ez Chaiim*, shows, the Jews scratched out and deleted certain passages in which he spoke of Jesus in such a way that they feared he might appear to be a Christian. However, the sublime knowledge of the Name of Him who is, who was, and who shall be (for that is what they call it), of the first three Sephiroth and of the seven other Sephiroth, which come together to form the number ten, and of the arrangement of the principles or successions or eternities that emerge from out of one another, or of why the world was not brought from the unmanifest into manifestation sooner; the knowledge of Adam Kadmon, of the lights, beams and vessels of light, of the bowls and vessels or containers shattered and congealed, in other words, knowledge of the Realm of Darkness, of the beings formed and made, of the separating of the outflowings and the works, of the wheels of Ezekiel, of the maternal waters above for the Restoration of the shattered vessels fallen into coarseness, indeed of prophecy and of the Holy Spirit, of the Transgression of Adam, and of innumerable other mysteries that would be intelligible only to faith: this whole system is of such venerable worth that no reasonable person could regard it as the play of fantasy.

These mysteries are veiled with images most obscure, selected from the anatomy of the human body. It is the true Seed of the eternal Word become flesh that they see, in piecemeal fashion, of course, in an obscure word scattered here and there. But in Jacob Boehme this sun is visible, even though in actual fact he had to draw his sketches in the black strokes of charcoal; and what is veiled by them is by him fully unveiled, so that even the weakest, since he has only a little patience and his concentration is broken and he follows the light under a cloud, may attain to the morning star and the bright noon day, indeed, to this sun in itself, because now are the Days of the Spirit." A remark of Oetinger's that is also characteristic is found in his *Conversation on the High Priesthood of Christ*, (1772, p. 162). In a discussion on the Christian doctrine of Redemption he says:

To help the fallen nature that has sunk into powerlessness, I have often recited from the work of the most learned Jew, Rabbi Isaac Luria, the *Cavanot Harij* (l. 40). In the appendix it reads as follows: 'In the time of the ten slaughtered for the kingdom, the transgressors had gained the upper hand to such an extent that there was no power among the children of Adam to make the feminine [light] water rise up so as to illumine through prayer the extinguished soul-sparks. Then must their children be put to death and their blood shed, so that in this way a power might glimmer again here below and become the rising of prayer to the Sanctuary.' From this, one may learn that the Jews themselves knew that powerlessness was to be met by nothing other than a new power of the blood that was shed. In this way I have convinced them that the Messiah must shed his blood in order to brighten again the sparks of the soul and bring a new power of life into the world.

47

VI.

OLD AND NEW KABBALAH

To understand the special form of F.C.Oetinger's
Christian Kabbalah, we need to review briefly
the development of the Jewish Kabbalah, which
culminated in Isaac Luria. The Jewish Kabbalah
passed through two significant and clearly distinct
phases. Within Jewish tradition, the second phase
bears the name New Kabbalah. This development

of the Kabbalah goes hand in hand with the fortunes of European and especially Spanish and Portugese Judaism. The year 1492 marks the decisive turning point. In this year, the Jews were expelled from Spain by the Catholic King, and were subjected to the uncertain fate of a new Exodus.

The Old Kabbalah consists more or less in the form of an esoteric teaching, limited to a small group of scholars, highly educated in religion and history, who placed no value on broader propaganda.[48] Characteristically in this older Kabbalah, the traditional messianic movements of Jewish religion, the deeply felt longing for the Advent of the Messiah, the coming of the Messianic Kingdom, the end of the world and the Renewal of the universe, were gradually replaced by speculation on the ur-origin of the world, on Creation's spiritual Image in God, and on the divine Ur-Image of Man in God.

In other words, the mystical meditations of these Kabbalists emphasized theogony and cosmogony rather than the history of salvation and Messianism; they were interested more in the ur-origin and beginning of the world than its end. Their contemplation was directed to the primordial Oneness of the world when the world still rests in the consciousness of God and from which it steps out into manifestation in the act of creation. This Oneness is seen as "the structure of the world before Satan's first rebellion." Thinking on creation takes precedence over thinking on redemption; or rather, the way of redemption is believed to lie specifically in contemplating the Ur-Oneness of the world in God, of the world in divine consciousness and of man in God, and of the Ur-Image of Man in divine consciousness, and of the way of meditation in "vision" participating in that Ur-Oneness and returning to it.

The great catastrophe of the year 1492 uprooted Spanish Judaism from the high culture of the Spanish world empire and threw it into the cruel insecurity of a new Exodus. This effected a powerful transformation in its religious consciousness, and created a New Kabbalah. Under the influence of this historical catastrophe, the messianic and eschatological elements of the Jewish religion, which were less developed in the older Kabbalah, surged again to the foreground, and became the focal point of an aggressive promotion. The catastrophe itself of 1492 came to be viewed as a symptom of the birth pangs of the Messianic era. From this time, the Kabbalah took on an entirely different form: it stepped out of the arena of mystical teaching and became an impulse for an active piety that shaped all the Jewish communities in their new dispersion.

The most important form of the New Kabbalah is that of Rabbi Isaac Luria, from whose school came the most important writings of the New Kabbalah. Of Isaac Luria himself, no original writings have come down. He was a visionary so inundated by spiritual perceptions that he could not hold them fast. When asked why he never wrote his thoughts down in book form, he replied: "That is impossible because everything runs together every which way. I can scarcely open my mouth to speak without feeling as though the sea has burst its dams and is overflowing. How can I describe what my soul has experienced, and how could I set it down in a book?"

The extant writings of Luria are actually reproductions of his talks with his students, coming from the pen of these students themselves. Among them, Hajim Vital and Rabbi Joseph ibn Tabul play an especially important role. Hajim Vital is also the author of the book that made such a great impression on Oetinger, *Ez Chaim* (Tree of Life). The Kabbalah of Luria was most widely dispersed through the work of another student, Israel Sarug, who promoted the New Kabbalah in a lively promotion among pious Italian Jews between 1592 and 1598.

Isaac Luria had a striking spiritual relationship with the great Christian visionary, Emmanuel Swedenborg, with whom he corresponded nearly his whole life, and whom Oetinger had discovered. Luria's writings also contain a series of rather very striking visions, in which he conducts a dialogue with the spirits of great wise men of the past. He frequently evoked the astonishment of his students when walking around with them in the neighborhood of Safed. Based on revelations he received from the spirits of pious men from the past, he would find their graves as they had revealed them to him.

There is without question a close, inner relationship between the New and the Old Kabbalah in Oetinger. Oetinger, of course, stands wholly in the eschatological tradition of Pietism. A disciple of Johann Albrecht Bengels, he belonged to that branch of Pietism whose eschatological expectation harkened back to the literal understanding of the End that characterized early Christianity, owing to Bengel's calculations of the Last

Day based on a special divine revelation. Oetinger was deeply convinced that the world was in fact rushing to its End at a tremendous pace, that the Return of Christ would in fact take place in the year 1834, and that the "Golden Age" would arrive in a few decades. Because of the proximity of the End, he felt obliged to urge the princes and government of his time to prepare the people for the "Golden Age" that was drawing near by putting into effect a courageous reform of rights and the social order, and so contribute to the speedy end of the world and its crossing over to the "Golden Age."

The highest dignitaries, of course, gave him no answer. But one or another of the less important dignitaries did. For example, the prince Johann Friedrich of Schwarzburg-Rudolstadt, to whom Oetinger had sent a copy of his *Golden Age*, answered Oetinger in a letter on Sept 25, 1760, and alluded to his Kabbalistic notions of the End-time. "I am much delighted hereby to make your acquaintance. The tractate on the *Golden Age*, which you were so kind to send to me, proves you possess an extensive knowledge of literature. It contains, as you know, a subject that evokes great controversy among the theologians. You maintain that the Church may hope for such a time, which you confirm from Holy Scripture as much as from empirical proofs. Allow me to add a single passage, found among those adduced by you on p. 5, which, as you say, Abarbanel accepts as proof of the Golden Age in his *Maschmia Jeschuah*. It is Deutermony 19:8-9. This prophecy promises much for Israel. Yet, if one compares it to the words God spoke to them through the angel in Judges 2.1, one learns that God prevented it from happening." (To this, Oetinger remarks: The pious prince commits the error of his theologians; he does not thoroughly examine the matter. This shows how even the most majestic marks of truth are placed in question in this age of skepticism. It will soon be enjoined, indeed it has already begun: "Fear God and give honor to him because the Time of his Judgment has come. Worship him who made the heavens, earth, and the fountains. Rev 14) "I admire the counsel you have given on how to prepare for this Golden Age as much as I do the organization of the best government. If all rulers would commit to this, and constantly keep this great goal before them, they would experience a fortune and a freedom almost comparable to that of the presupposed Golden Age. For my part, I shall make every effort to implement your book and to edify myself with its vision."[49]

Thus, Christian Kabbalism received in Oetinger a strong eschatological thrust. For him, all things are seen as omens vindicating the expectation that burns strongly for the imminent Second Coming of Christ, for the descent of the heavenly Jerusalem, the eschatological installation of the high priesthood of Christ, the beginning of the "Golden Age," the Transformation of fallen Humanity and its Restoration in the Image of the Humanity raised and renewed in Christ.

VII.

THE KABBALISTIC MASTER TABLET OF PRINCESS ANTONIA

Oetinger's professional activity in Wurttemberg, when he was at the height of his literary career, brought him for a third time into contact with the Kabbalah in an unexpected manner. This was the Christian Kabbalah of the Kabbalistic Tablet of Princess Antonia, to whose interpretation Oetinger devoted an entire book.[50] Our prelate of Herrenberg came upon this Kabbalistic Tablet in the region of the Wurttemberg Church itself, in a neglected mural that for a century had been gathering dust in the Church of neighboring Nirsau. Oetinger's encounter with the Kabbalistic Tablet can be traced back to the time well before 1759, as indicated in his sermons. During his time in Herrenberg, Oetinger was so full of Kabbalistic ideas that he was not afraid to preach his Christian Kabbalah to his community from the Sunday pulpit, and he even wrote down such Kabbalistic sermons in his collection of sermons, which appeared in 1759 under the title, *Reden nach dem allgemeinen Wahrheitsgefühl über die sonntäglichen Evangelia vom Advent bis auf Trinitatis und die Feiertage* [*Talks in pursuit of the Universal sense of Truth on the Sunday Gospels from the Feast Days of Advent to the Trinity*].

In that collection of sermons, his sermon delivered on the Feast of the Three Wise Men, where he deals with the story of Nicodemus (Jn 3:1-5), is in particular thoroughly Kabbalistic in content. In this sermon he even goes so far as to accept the Kabbalistic doctrine which maintains that the Kabbalah was present among men from the beginning of the world as a ur-revelation, revealing to mankind the Way of Salvation. The text is as follows:

Accordingly, we are earnest in our desire to show you what enjoyment of eternal life there is for those who have within themselves the fruitful knowledge of the Trinity. There are many among the heathens, the Jews, and the Christians who have within themselves the blessed enjoyment of eternal life because their sight is illumined by communion with God. Nicodemus was a master in Israel. Without doubt, he knew a good deal of the Trinity from the common teaching of the Jews. He knew the ten radiances or Sefiroth from the book of Abraham, called *Sefer Yezirah*, which is really the doctrine of the Trinity. He knew from Micah (5:1) that the outgoing of the Kingly Messiah would be from the beginning and from eternity. Of these outflowings or radiances or Sephiroth, the Jews counted ten, or three times three plus one, just as the holy *Apocalypse* enumerates three and seven (1.4). There are however only three which dwell in the lower and higher regions, or two times three, and these are joined in the ten.

Oetinger therefore counted Nicodemus as a master of the Kabbalah who knew already the mystery of the Trinity underlying the Kabbalistic doctrine of the Sefiroth, and who joined the Kabbalistic doctrine of the ten Sefiroth to the dogma of the Three and the seven spirits, of which the *Apocalypse* of John speaks.[51] Most astonishing, however, is that Oetinger publicly states in a sermon that this primal revelation of the divine Outflowings found in the Kabbalah was known even before Christ. He boldly explains that those Jews and heathen who possessed the Kabbalah and "saw from their communion with God," which means that their "vision" was informed by their communion with God, "are partakers of eternal life [theosis]." In the same sermon, Oetinger identifies Nicodemus' Kabbalistic vision of God with the vision of God found in the book of the *Zohar*. He must therefore have believed that Nicodemus was a contemporary of Rabbi Simeon ben Jochai, the author, in his opinion, of the *Zohar*. He goes on to say: "Students of Rabbi Simeon asked their master: 'If there are two and there is one, then there are three. If there are three, how can there be one?' (*Zohar*, part iii. p. 162)

Other Kabbalists call it "the higher Synetrium" since Three are together up there in the Upper region

(*Schaare Ora* p. 41b, line 7). The Kabbalist Nicodemus, so Oetinger affirms, "knew all this already," except that his knowledge of the Triad was "yet unfruitful." His meeting with Jesus did not impart new knowledge to him; it simply made the Kabbalistic knowledge of God he already possessed fruitful. Here, the Christian Kabbalah's vision of God appears as that which makes the Jewish Kabbalah's vision of God alive and active. As an example of this Christian Kabbalah, Oetinger adduced Princess Antonia, whose Kabbalistic Tablet he briefly summarized in the same sermon:

Between 1613 and 1679, there lived in Stuttgart two princesses of Wurtemberg, Anna Johanna and Antonia. Both sisters were great aunts of the most illustrious and esteemed princess Friederika of Wurtemberg, still living, whose piety God will crown with power and grace. While Anna Johanna was thoroughly grounded in the sciences, Princess Antonia loved only the Holy Bible and the Kabbalah that dealt with the Sefiroth in the *Zohar*. She loved the Kabbalah not from curiosity. She had greatly yearned to understand the Triad after the ancient Jewish manner in the 10 Sefiroth. She was instructed in the Hebrew language, and saw indeed that two and two radiances are united in the third, in love and severity, and goodness and sincerity, in keenness and gentleness. She also saw in the figure of the crucified Jesus, foreshadowed in the raising up of the serpent, three (Sefiroth) in the head, three in the breast and shoulders, three in the hip and stomach, and all were united in the tenth (Sefiroth) as in the realm of the King (Malkuth). These bring together and unite the whole mystery of God and Christ, indeed the entire Old and New Testaments, and she had a very edifying painting done of it in the mineral springs of the Church in Teinach, and had

57

her heart buried in it. One would wish that both nobility and commoners would have such joy as to taste eternal life in these truths, and to have its connection with all truths graphically set before them, as it were.[52]

The fact that the Kabbalah gained its entrance into the Sunday sermon itself is a surer sign of genuine encounter between Judaism and Christianity, as would be attained only at rare outposts in Church history, than any purely academic and esoteric connection of Christian theology with the Kabbalah.

In the years after 1759, Oetinger occupied himself even more intensively with the Master Tablet. The work that he published in the meantime showed that Jacob Friedrich Klemm, a frequent benefactor from Tubingen, wrote a letter to him from Stuttgart on 21 July, 1763. In it, he reported to Oetinger that he "not long ago saw the remarkable Tablet of the whole Kabbalistic doctrine in the Church in Bad Teinach, and was immediately possessed of a deep desire to be thoroughly instructed on it. Who now is more qualified to give me such instruction than your high reverence, which has achieved an insight most rare in our time, through your many years of association with the Kabbalists, and your own untiring research into the secret doctrine of the Jews?"

Oetinger appears in this letter, published in the introduction of his work, as one of the few existing Christian scholars of the Kabbalah who comes immediately to mind as one who can interpret the Kabbalistic Master Tablet. Klemm further reports that he considered "the matter of such value that it should be published and a detailed sketch of the entire painting should be made, to bring it to the attention of today's scholars." He went on to say that he had already made a sketch of the tablet himself, and then proceeds to describe the Master Tablet in detail.

So what is it about? Let us note at once that although the Kabbalistic Master Tablet still exists today in the Church of Bad Teinach, to the best of my knowledge no one has troubled himself to study this rare monument until most recently. It is called, "The Master Tablet of Princess Antonia," because it was donated by Antonia, Princess of Wurtemburg, a sister of Duke Eberhard III, daughter of Johann Friedrichs, Duke of Wurtemburg. She lived from March 24, 1613 to October 1, 1679. Her special relationship to this gift comes to light in her directive to have her heart removed from her body after her death and to have it entombed under this Tablet, and this is what happened. All three daughters of Duke Johann Friedrich were uncommonly gifted. Princess Anna Johanna was a great admirer of art; Princess Sibylla a learned expert of historical and genealogical sciences.

The particular inclination of Princess Antonia, however, was applied to theology, and in particular to the Kabbalah. How she came to it, from what underground stream of the Kabbalistic tradition she drew at the beginning of the 17th century, neither she nor Oetinger say. This only is sure: she was instructed in the Hebrew language by M. Johann Jacob Strehlin, evangelical pastor of Munster in Stuttgart. Beyond that, she had a connection with another expert of the Hebraic and rabbinic traditions, Rev. J.L.Schmidhin from Sindelfingen, whose sermons she attended from her temporary residence in Ehningen. The third Hebraist in her personal circle was Professor Raith from the University of Tubingen, who was the Princess's teacher of dogma.

Nothing more can be determined about which of the three teachers initiated the princess in the esoteric doctrines of the Kabbalah. We can be sure only that Prof. Raith, at the consecration of the image on the Feast of the Trinity in the year 1673, gave a speech on the "Master Tablet that springs from the Tree of the Kabbalistic mystery," which appeared in print in Tubingen in 1673 under the title *Turris Antonia oder Einweihungsrede bei Aufrichtung der in der Kirche in Deinach gestifteten Lehrtafel* [*Turris Antonia, or Consecration at the Raising Up of the Master Tablet donated to the Church in Teinach*].

The ostensible occasion for the donation of the image was the laying of the cornerstone of the Church in Bad Teinach by the benefactress' brother, Duke Eberhard III, in the year 1662. At that time, Princess Antonia resolved to give a tablet for the Church of the Trinity in Teinach, on which was "graphically depicted the profoundest doctrine of the Hebraic philosophy;" "to give honor to the true God and to no other, for the adornment of this Church, for the good pleasure of my highly learned, my most honored and dearly beloved brother, for a pledge of grace to the inhabitants of this place, and for unceasing contemplation to those recently arrived from other places."

Oetinger himself dedicated his explanation of the Tablet to the visitors of Teinach and the nearby mineral baths. Moreover, in his explanation he notes that here will be "explained the power of the well-springs for the philosophy of the Hebrews, the Spirit of God, according to all passages of the New Testament." He himself explained that with the Tablet, the princess wanted to offer:

A graphic sermon, both to visitors and to all of Wurttemberg: First, of the Threefoldness, which holy revelation expressed in the Kabbalist manner according to the three Self-standings of the Standings of God—that which is, which was, and which shall be. Second, of the Seven Spirits of God, so that three and seven are depicted on two columns as ten persons, outgoing into a house above and below, centered on Christ in an oval shaped garden. Third, of Christ, who stands at the center of the garden.

It would require an entire series of lectures to explain this Tablet. Indeed, we saw that Oetinger himself wrote an entire book on it. Here, we may highlight only a few points.

1. Under discussion here is what already is a Christian Kabbalah. That means a Kabbalah for which the conception of the Messiah as the Renewer of the Ur-Man, of the Divine Man, of the Divine Ur-Image of Man in Jesus Christ, which is included in the Kabbalistic expectation of the End-times, had already been fulfilled initially, and will find its complete fulfillment in the Messiah's coming again. What Pico de la Mirandola had maintained in his *Conclusions* – namely that: "no science proves the Divinity of Christ as well as the Kabbalah and Magia," – is depicted here in all detail and graphic clarity.

2. On purely literary historical grounds, the

significance of Oetinger's explanation lies in the fact that here for the first time he conveys to a Christian theological readership the whole system of the Kabbalah, and so, shortly before his death, he crowned his life-long efforts to understand the Kabbalah. At the same time, he used this opportunity to familiarize his contemporaries fully with the content of the book, *Zohar*. The work begins with a translation of the "passages from the *Zohar* on the philosophy of the Hebrews, according to an excerpt of Lord M. Sommers, *Lat. Specimen Theologiae Soharicae*." In 21 paragraphs, he sets forth the whole system of the *Zohar* with its different teachings on God, on the Sefiroth, on the World, Primordial Man, the Fall, Redemption, the Messiah, and the Consummation of the Kingdom of God.

3. Even more significant, Kabbalistic philosophy is compared to the major philosophical and theological systems of the time. Indeed, it is raised as a criterion for all philosophy and theology of the time. Thus, we find, to name only a few chapters (pp. 88ff.), "A Comparison of Newtonian Philosophy with the Kabbalistic," where in each case the philosophy of Jacob Boehme is advanced as a second criterion next to the Kabbalah. As we see, it is Oetinger's idea, implanted in him by Koppel Hecht, that in Boehme the Kabbalah attains to its highest level, and is developed in all completeness. Then follows as chapter 3, p. 91ff., a "Comparison of Wolf's philosophy with the Kabbalah;" chapter 4, p. 92ff., "Lord Professor Plouquet's System compared to the Kabbalah;" chapter 5, a comparison with Detlev Cluver's system, including a "Comparison

with Jacob Boehme's Kabbalah;" chapter 6, with Swedenborg's system; chapter 7, with the philosophy of Baglivius, and in an appendix, a comparison with the philosophy of Frederick the Great, "the philosophy of *sans souci* [letting-go]." There then follows an explanation of the "Doctrine of the Prophet Ezekiel on the Soul and Intelligences," p. 117 ff., and finally a metaphysical apology of Jacob Boehme's system under the title, "New Metaphysical Reflections on the Kabbalistic System, from which the Ten Outflowings of God become conceivable." Then follows the New Testament foundation of these doctrines in the form of a detailed exegesis of New Testament passages on the "Holy Spirit" and on the Glory or Lordliness of God. Finally, Oetinger adds an excerpt from the manuscript of the "most illustrious and highly learned Princess Antonia, found in the written legacy of her teacher, Rev. Strelin," who composed in the Hebrew language a "sketch of the ultimate sources of all created things, i.e. of the Sefiroth," p. 229ff. He also includes some illustrations of the Master Tablet, which come from Princess Antonia herself and were drawn by Rev. Schmidhin. Oetinger himself also refers to a manuscript of Schmidhin's with the title, "Tit. Enyclopedia Turris Antonia erectae ab Celsissima et Serenissima Principe ac Domina, Domina Antonia, Duce Wurtenbergiae, descripta a Joh. Laurention Schmidhin" (Tower of Antonia, erected by the most illustrious and serene founder and Mistress, the Mistress Antonia, Dutchess of Wurtemberg, described by Joh. Laurention Schmidhin). Oetinger notes in regard to this: "In addition, there stands underneath:

'These tablets were diligently sorted and arranged according to the customary order in the princely consistory, and impressions of them were made in Stuttgart, Dec. 18, 1663; they remained unpublished, however."

VIII.

OETINGER'S DOCTRINE OF THE SEFIROTH

Finally, we can illustrate the substance of Kabbalistic speculation by describing briefly the doctrine of the Sefiroth, which is also at the center of the Christian Kabbalah. In considering these ideas, one must constantly remember that we are not dealing with abstract speculations or logical concepts, but with an effort to give expression to religious intuitions and experiences. The creators of the Kabbalah were not abstract thinkers; they were mystics, men of prayer, and in large part ascetics who spent their life in prayerful meditation and contemplation on the mysteries of God.

The thought of these men was dominated by two fundamental impulses: first, the feeling of a sacred and sublime transcendence of God that plumbs the deepest depths, a sense that feels in highest measure the holiness of God, the *tremendum* and *fascinosum* of God. Second, this piety was practiced with the consciousness that this holy God and this earthly world are intimately linked together. They did not see the world as separated from God, nor did they identify it with God, but they were profoundly convinced that God is present in this world in both its smallest and greatest things, and they sought to comprehend this God present in the world under the viewpoint of the beginning and the end. Thus, their main contemplation was applied to the questions: how did the world come forth from God, how were God and the world joined to one another causally and essentially; and further, what does God intend for this world which he governs so powerfully and deeply, and to what goal is he guiding this world? This piety was all the more convinced of God's constant presence in the world because it was predominantly visionary and this presence of the sacred in the world was manifest to them in manifold visionary forms and intuitive experiences.

Only if one keeps these fundamental religious presuppositions in mind is one able to grasp the particulars of Kabbalistic teachings. The doctrine of the Sefiroth is nothing other than the attempt to understand God's self-unfolding, to which the beginning and development of the universe and of man are directly and essentially connected on their various levels. Presupposed in this regard is a conception of the divine Being, which the Kabbalists derive, with a tremor that is always fresh and most profoundly felt, from the interpretation of God's Name revealed by Moses to the Holy from out of the burning bush in the Wilderness: "I Am Who I Am." God's Being is an unfathomable will toward self-revelation, a longing or thrust toward *manifestatio sui* [self-manifestation] as Oetinger would say, a longing to step out of his unfathomable depths and to actualize himself. As the mirrored-splendors and outflowings of God, the Sefiroth are different levels on the way to self-mirroring and self-manifestation of the transcendent divine Being.

The doctrine of the Sefiroth therefore basically describes nothing other than the levels of a theogony, except that the theogonic process here is transposed to the divine Being itself. In this process, it attains not only to consciousness, but also to an embodiment of itself.

Since in this process, the self-manifestation of God includes also his self-manifestation in the creation of the universe, and his self-imaging in man as the Image of God and thereby the whole salvation history of mankind, both the development of the world as well as salvation history itself are included in this process of God's self-manifestation, which is accomplished throughout by the Sefiroth. Not only the development of the universe, but salvation history as well is a theogonic process.

From this basic assumption, perhaps we can understand the Outflowings of the Sefiroth doctrine through Oetinger's explanations and interpretations of the *Kabbalistic Master Tablet* in order to answer the question, "How should one explain in a simple way the doctrine of the ten Outflowings of God?" In his answer, Oetinger points first to those basic concepts we have just mentioned. "God is the unfathomable

Depth, the *En Sof*, which on the Tablet stands above, dwelling in itself: this desires to impart itself to or to be in participation with Creation. Therefore, the first outflowing out of the *En Sof*, out of the *Ungrund*, is called *in the beginning*, as we pray in the hymn: 'To the triune God: as he was in the beginning, so he is and ever shall be, now and forevermore.'" Here, God shines forth as the unfathomable Depth, as the *Ungrund*, which thrusts itself out of itself in order to communicate itself, a conception that strongly influenced the theology of the late Schelling, who also described the inmost being of God as the "Ungrund," which is for God essentially a will toward self-manifestation.[53]

Throughout, it is presupposed that the Being of God, as it rests in its *Ungrund*, is a fullness that contains in itself an endlessness of Life and Spirit (*Master Tablet*, p. 14): "If it seems strange to the natural man that there should be ten outflowings of God, then let him consider that Holy Scripture speaks of a fullness of God; therefore, of something that is fulfilled through many emanations or outflowings of God."

The deep inner connection between the theology of Schelling and the Kabbalistic idea of God is illuminating for the history of literature in that Schelling comes not only from the theological tradition of the Tubingen theological school, in which the ideas of Oetinger thrived, but also in that his philosophy of antiquity preceded a spontaneous rediscovery of Oetinger's theosophy, in which he encountered a Christian transposition of the Kabbalistic doctrine of God.[54]

According to Oetinger, the *first* Sefira, [*Keter*] the Crown, represents an inner emergence to the self-manifestation of God: "Through the first, God steps forth as a crown, or as an immeasurable peripheral outbranching of his inner points (Ps 150.1), or as a concentration to his self-manifestation."

The form of Wisdom, *Hochmah*, in which "he beholds himself," represents the *second* step of God's self-manifestation. Here, Oetinger enters into a complex Wisdom speculation, which illumines this level of divine self-manifestation in a detailed manner very similar to that of Jacob Boehme. On this step, God comes to consciousness of himself, after he has concentrated, on the first step, on the self-manifestation of himself.

This act in which God becomes conscious of himself is the presupposition for the *third* step of self-manifestation (*Binah* [Understanding]), in which he "gives himself over to the separation of the original, pre-worldly ideas in himself." In this act of becoming self-conscious, God will clarify the inner fullness of his Being. The individual Original-ideas of divine consciousness step forth into their separating-out. Wisdom "plays before God" (Prov 8.31), which means, she lets the whole fullness of the Original-ideas blaze up playfully in the divine consciousness, so that a separating springs up in him himself. "The Holy Spirit separates the Hiddenness of Wisdom through the 2 in 3, and through these in seven, and even further to infinity (Job 11.6)."

The *fourth* form (*Gedulah* or *Chesed* [Love or Mercy]) signifies now that step of the divine self-manifestation in which God "out-spreads his powers in himself." (Ps 150.1). "Praise him in the out-branching of his power."

The reference to the word from Psalm 150.1 would be confusing to the reader of Luther's translation, because there it reads: "Praise the Lord in his sanctuary, praise him in the firmness of his might." Oetinger, however, here keeps to the Hebraic text and translates it in the Rabbinic sense: "Praise him in the branching out of his strength," and, like Newton, Leibniz and Schelling after him, adds to this word his own speculations on space.[55] Space is the "sensorium dei" (the seat of God's sensation), the outbranching of his Might, in which the inmost point of the divine Being stretches out to its endless periphery. In this sense, this particular Psalm passage is used in the explanation of the *Master Tablet of Antonia* in his speculations on space, and brings it directly in line with Newton's doctrine on space. For example, in his chapter, "Comparison of Newtonian Philosophy with the Kabbalistic,"[56] one reads: "1. God is present from within and from without with his substance. 2. God is present in and through the central powers. 3. These branch out in endless space (Ps 150.4). 4. This space is the *Sensorium* of God (Ps 150). 5. This space is empty of matter, yet full of Spirit (Ps 150)Ö15. In eternal space, God is all in all."

What Newton calls the central powers, Oetinger develops in his teaching on the Spirit. The Spirit of God is a unified Spirit. He specifies himself, however, by the number seven, and so it can easily be implied from all flowers, herbs, stones, and animals, that an all-universal unified Spirit of nature goes out to the sanctuary of heaven, filling up the space of heaven (Ps 150.1) and itself in seven powers and thereafter through combinations, *conternationes* (placing of three things together), *conquaternationes* (placing of four things together) in endless corporeal and specific mixtures."[57]

This "outbranching of his strength (Ps 150.1) is the proto-groundoutsetting of God's manifestation to the creature. God cannot manifest himself to the creature as he dwells in himself in his *Ungrund*. For God cannot be considered apart from the outbranching of his strength (Ps 150.1), without some element or without a spiritual center of movement in the element. It is the God and Father of Splendor who brings forth his splendor from himself according to his good pleasure." In this splendor, "God is neither without space, nor time, nor self-movement, nor passivity and receptivity, nor reflection, nor radiance, nor circulation of powers. In short, whatever properties are found in the creature, such as those pertaining to the organism, viz., bodily shape and transformation, these same attributes and no less are also found in the Spirit of God."[58]

The full explanation of this Psalm passage reads: "The Splendor of God is not God himself, but rather the Light wherein he dwells (Ps 104.2; I Tim 6.16), and is called *Rakia uesso*, the outstretching of his strength (Ps 150.1), in which are understood the Overcoming-powers, *Gebhurot*, and the outgoing of the Father of Lights. In this outgoing are found the overcoming-powers, the lights, the outgoings, the things not seen (Hebr 11.3), the αορατα, the invisible things of God (Rom 1.20), the αιδιος δυναμις, the eternal

70

Power, and according to Job 11.6, the Hiddenness of Wisdom...This *expansum* is passive, and receives all forms, which the Active or eternal Word gives to it through the central powers, which are the or-origin of the circular movement. (Eze 1.4; Prov 8.27)."⁵⁹

On the *fifth* step of God's self-manifestation (*Gevura* or *Din*) [Judgment or Power]), "he intends and composes his powers together again, so that we praise him in his *Gebhurot* or powers (Ps 150.1)." The fourth and fifth steps, therefore, form as well the level of expansion and contraction, in which God becomes conscious of his fullness in the Struggle of his individually separated ideas and powers.

On the *sixth* step (*Tiphereth* [Compassion]), "from out of the Struggle, he brings extension and intension into bodily beauty, as the Psalmist sings: "Praise adorns him and beauty is in his sanctuary (Ps 96.6)."

On the *seventh* step (*Netsah* [Endurance-victory or Eternity]), "he overcomes, so that the struggle of the consuming powers passes over into that which is received in the victory (*Lanazach*) of pure act (*actu purissimo*)." The movement on the preceding steps sets out that in God himself a contrary-struggle primordially-plays-out between consuming and receiving powers, that in the divine Being itself a struggle takes place, which forms the presupposition for the proto-processes of separating-out and of becoming self-conscious. "As, no doubt, there is no transition in God from strife to rest, nevertheless, he does not say without reason that he rested. So the active powers and the outgoings of God continue to go out until they come to rest. There is no change in

71

God; yet he is an eternal *actus* which proceeds to rest, an eternal moving in stillness."

"Through the *eighth* step, *Hod,* Splendor, there is a drawing near to rest. Splendor is the basic word of the New Testament in which all things shall increase (II Cor 3). This is the Kabbalah of Paul."

In the *ninth* step, *Yesod* [Foundation], "All things become their existence or standing." This step is "the fountain-source of all sentient perception and apperception." (*Swedenborg and Other Philosophies of Earth and Heaven*, Frankfurt/Leipzig, 1765, p. 345). "All sensate things, all reflections, all powers, the immortality of the soul, all things that endure and that receive existence have their root here. A rock is God; therefore, his work is perfect." (Dt. 32.4)

On the *tenth* step, *Malkhut* [Kingdom], the self-unfolding of God attains its goal and its completion. Here, "the Godhead comes to the entelechy of pure act, i.e. a passing-over to rest, to eternal equanimity, to Sabbath, to Kingdom, and that means to Adonai, to the Lord of all Lords, Christ, a passing-over that is active and progressive. There the Godhead betakes itself to a new, hidden from eternal time, standing-forth for humanity and angels. Then, the mystery of God becomes also the mystery of Christ." On this step, divine self-manifestation thrusts on to its embodiment, to its bodiliness. According to the well-known formulas of Oetinger, which Schelling also adopted, "Embodiment is the end of all the ways of God;"[60] and, "Embodiment is not incompleteness, but, rather, completeness."[61]

Oetinger understood the doctrine of the Sefiroth as

the Kabbalah's most important contribution to the knowledge of Christian theology. "Since salvation comes from the Hebrews, so must one receive the good in its teaching; in particular, its teaching on the properties or fountain powers of God or the Sefiroth .. . No schoolmaster has seen these who has not studied in the school of the Hebrews."[62] He saw the special importance of this doctrine to lie in the fact that it completed and illumined the Christian doctrine of the Trinity. To him, it seemed to give a deeper insight into the inner movement of God's self-manifestation than was possible in the Christian dogma of the Trinity. In his opinion, the Kabbalistic doctrine of the ten Sefiroth encompassed within itself the Christian doctrine of the Trinity, but contained as well further disclosures on the unfolding of the divine Life in the universe and in salvation history.

This connection of the Christian doctrine of the Trinity to the Kabbalistic doctrine of the Sefiroth belongs to the oldest tradition of the Christian Kabbalah. In the Swabian tradition of the Christian Kabbalah, it formed Reuchlin's main concern in his two writings, *De Verbo mirificio*, 1494, and *De arte Cabbalistica*, 1516.[63] As chief evidence for the existence of the Kabbalistic doctrine of the ten Sefiroth in Christian theology, Oetinger draws attention to the passage from John's *Apocalypse* 1.4-5, where it says: "Of Him who is, who was, and who shall be," and of the "seven spirits." Basically, in his interpretation of the evangelist John, Oetinger asserts that it was dedicated to the teachings of the Kabbalah, and that it was written in a Kabbalistic style. In this regard, he refers to the work of Rhenferd, which in his time had created quite a stir and bore the title: *De stilo Cabbalistico Johannis* (*The Kabbalistic Style of John*).[64] In his *Master Tablet*, he explains this passage from the *Apocalypse* of John 1.4-5 in the following way:

We may surely understand that in the Holy Scripture it does not mean: 'The triune God greets you,' but that there are two greetings: one from the three and the seven, and a special greeting that proceeds from Jesus Christ. From this, it is clear that He who is, was, and shall be, is portrayed under three manifestations, which the Kabbalists call Sefiroth, and that the other seven complete the number of the ten outflowings, and that consequently, the Third Person greets us under the particular form of the Seven. Furthermore, it is clear that the Messiah looks upon himself in particular as Man, and that He is the Alpha and Omega in union and communion with the ten Sefiroth in his union with Mankind, just as the eternal God is the Alpha and Omega outside of humanity.[65]

From these ten Sefiroth, the first three form a special group and signify the Trinity, while the other seven are the seven spirits and spirit-fountains of God. "The first three Sefiroth, the All-Holy Crown, the Wisdom, and the Understanding, are inseparably united to one another and signify the Threeness of Persons in the Divine Being. The All-Holy Crown is the uppermost, supreme Sefira, or the First Person of the Godhead. Wisdom is the second Person, the Son of God, Logos or Word. Understanding is the Third Person, the Holy Spirit, because he explores the depths of the Godhead as the third so-called Person."[66] The expression, "so-called Person" shows that such an identification of the Kabbalistic doctrine of the Sefiroth cannot be sustained without certain repercussions for the orthodox understanding of the Trinity. In the final analysis, the Kabbalistic doctrine of the Sefiroth is connected to the neo-Platonic doctrine of emanations. The Sefiroth are emanations, outpourings, mirrored-splendors, rays of the divine *Ungrund*, which contains in itself an immeasurable fullness of life, but not Persons in the sense of the classical doctrine of the Trinity.

Koppel Hecht earlier had pointed out to the young Oetinger that he could not agree with the doctrine of the Christian Church because of its strangeness. Specifically, the Christian doctrine of the Trinity, in the sense of a Oneness of Three Persons, formed for Jewish piety, firmly rooted in the concept of the Oneness of God, a constant difficulty and appeared as a distortion of the inviolable doctrine of the absolute Oneness of God. Accordingly, one finds among the Christian Kabbalists a tendency to interpret the doctrine of the Three Persons of God in a modalistic sense. This means that the Three Persons are understood as forms of the realization, manifestation and actualization of the One God. In a very similar manner, Oetinger says in his *Dictionary of Emblems*: "Although there is in God a three-fold work or act in himself, through himself, and out of himself, even so, one cannot call this a person." "Wisdom is the proto-image of the invisible Being, which is eternally born from it. There may be, then, only two: God and Word, God and Wisdom. Wisdom is somewhat visible and is called the Angel of the Covenant. In himself, God

75

is invisible. In Wisdom, the beginning of the creature comes into view as the angel. The outflowing from Wisdom through the Spirit towards the creation and the return to God, the Eternal One, is the Spirit."[67]

It is significant also that Oetinger in his *Master Tablet* expressly insists that one should not impose on the Jews the Doctrine of the three Persons. "One must exempt the Jews only from the word, person, and replace it with outflowing or mirrored-splendor or sefiroth. It is enough that we say with them that in the Godhead there are three outflowings, which go back into One and are One. Any particular outflowing may be a special understanding-power. The first, second and third have each their own autonomy."[68] Here, the Christian doctrine of the Trinity is joined to the Jewish doctrine of the Sefiroth. The doctrine of the Three Persons is replaced by the doctrine of the three "Outflowings" of the Godhead. Each of these outflowings has its own "self-standingness," and of course Oetinger's thought used the term Person for this self-standingness.

In the final analysis, the Christian doctrine of the Trinity is for Oetinger the expression of the same reality that he finds also expressed in the doctrine of the Sefiroth: that in the *Ungrund* of God, an incomprehensible overflowing, a superabundance of divine Life is contained that thrusts towards its actualization on various steps and cadences, and desires to realize its hidden manifoldness in a bodily way. The divine Triad is in realization an uncreated thousand-fold myriad. The three are the first forms of the radiance and actualization of the divine Life, in which God becomes conscious of himself, of his own inner fullness and the particular ways of his manifestation. "God is a particular I-ness, so also is the Word, so also is the Holy Spirit. This does not mean, however, that these three are one according to an arithmetical understanding. When it says in I John 5.3, "Three are one," this is not the one of arithmetic, but the true One (John 17). Outwardly, it is indeed one, but inwardly it is a myriad, an ingrasping of the hidden many that stand-out from the One and exist in the One."[69]

Here, it is clear that the entire doctrine of the Trinity is for him based in the final analysis on the idea of *life*, and that this primary thought of the "indissoluble bond of divine Life" has its origin in the thought that Oetinger holds in harmony with the Jewish Kabbalah and also the Christian Kabbalah of Jacob Boehme. The Being of God ultimately is a powerful, uncreated desire or will, a moving-fountain that is thrusting toward the manifestation, representation and embodiment of itself.

Seen as a whole, this interpretation naturally leads the orthodox doctrine of the Trinity, in the sense of the Kabbalistic doctrine of the Sefiroth, into considerable difficulties. Fundamentally, the Christian doctrine of the three-in-one is replaced by the Kabbalistic doctrine of a ten-in-one. And, it is arbitrary to join the first three Sefiroth together as a special group, on the basis of an exegetical artifice, and to relate them to the three-in-one. For this, Oetinger finds a rather complicated justification: "The Triad is beyond thought. The Sevenness is a two-fold Dwelling of the Triad, united in the Oneness. However, in the number 7, the Triad gives in its splendor a certain measure of powers, even though the splendor of God is without measure."[70]

The number seven $(10 = 3 + 2 \cdot 3 + 1)$ means that the seven spirits or outflowings represent therefore the "measure of the powers" in which the measureless splendor of the divine Triad is contained and circumscribed. However, even the seventh Sefira, which in the whole forms the tenth, creates only a new difficulty. In it, whose name is *Malkhut* [Kingdom], the self-movement of the Godhead comes to rest in Christ and his realm. This Sefira of necessity, then, should stand in a definite relationship to the second, *Hochmah*, which designates the Son of God. The fullness of the Godhead, which in its eternal movement of life is manifested through the three and through the seven Sefiroth, dwells in Christ. Yet, of a Three in One in the traditional churchly sense, there is no more word.

To be sure, Oetinger says in the explanation referred to above that "the Third Person greets us under the particular form of the seven spirits." But a new difficulty and confusion arises from this. Oetinger himself finally confirms that it is simply impossible to hold fast to a real distinction of Persons in the Trinitarian relationship. What he brings to expression in his joining of the classical doctrine of the Trinity with the doctrine of the Sefiroth is a speculative attempt to penetrate into the inner movement of life in the Godhead, and to comprehend the processes in the universe and in salvation history, the presence of God in the world, in nature, in humanity, and the various forms of the personal encounter between God and man from out of the inner movement of life in the Godhead itself. Also, the Christian Trinity doctrine is but the intellectual reflection, the insufficient attempt of human expression, a genuinely intuitive encounter with the divine Transcendence on the ground of its various forms of self-manifestation returning back to man.

IX.

CONCLUSION

Oetinger, whose theological thought was inspired by genuinely intuitive encounters with the Transcendent, clearly felt that the Kabbalistic doctrine of the Sefiroth shared the same concern to explain conceptually the mysterious phases of the self-actualization, manifestation and embodiment of the inner fullness of the Godhead, which also profoundly moved him. He therefore was not afraid to join the two doctrines together, and even to base this identity on bold exegesis. It would be a mistake to require dogmatic correctness of such an attempt. It is much more the expression of an experience of the Transcendent that formed a genuine community. We ourselves are not afraid to call it mystical, so long as this word is not weighed down by a multitude of misunderstandings and prejudices, and we can say with certainty that it was an experience of the Transcendent in which the greatest pious men of the Jews and Christians experienced themselves as one.

That appreciation of this commonality is on the rise again today confirms to me the conclusion in Leopold Ziegler's *Conversation of the Masters*, the most recent work of the great revivalist of Schelling's theology in our time. His *Conversations of the Masters on Universal Man*, at the climax of its presentation, joins the theogonic and eschatological aspects of the Image of the Universal Man, and in so doing comes upon the

Hasidic Image of the Messiah. There, Leopold Ziegler writes *apropos* his meditation on Hasidism concerning the Jewish capacity for Spirit: "There is a capacity for Spirit, moreover, which at the very least encompasses the Christian revelation as far as possible, and includes rather than excludes it in itself. I repeat: at the very least, as far as possible. Accordingly, I place all my hopes on that day of reconciliation, when Judaism and Christianity commonly acknowledge their guilt in their divisions and both affirm their common root in the symbol of the Return or Restoration."[71]

BIBLIOGRAPHIC NOTES

1.   Literature on the Christian Kabbalah:
Briman, Aron, *Die Kabbala und ihr Verhältnis zum Christentum*, 1885.

Hamberger, Julius, *Christenthum und moderne Cultur. Studien, Kritiken und Charakterbilder*, Nr. IX: *Die Kabbalah* (1846), (Erlangen: 1863).

Idem, *Die hohe bedeutung der altjüdischen Tradition oder der sogenannten Kabbalah*, (Sulzbach: 1844) (Reprint of the recension of *Molitors Philosophie der Geschichte* in *Münchner Gelehrten Anzeigen*).

Köster, Adolph, *Nachweis der Spuren der Trinitätslehre vor Christo*, (Frankfurt am Main: 1845).

Levi, Eliphas, *Les origins cabbalistiques du christianisme*, Paris.

Molitor, Franz Joseph, *Philosophie der Geschichte oder Über die Tradition*, 1. Vol. (Frankfurt am Main: 1827), vollst. umgearbeitet 1855, 2 Vol. (Münster: 1834), 3. Vol. (Münster: 1839), 4 Vol. (Münster: 1853).

Newman, Louis J., *Jewish Influence on Christian Reform Movements*, 1925.

Pick, Bernhard, *The Cabala*, 1913.

Scholem, Gershom, *Zur Geschichte der Anfänge der christlichen Kabbala, Tribute to Leo Baeck*, 1954.

Schulze, Wilhelm August, *Jacob Boehme und die Kabbala*, in: *Judaica*, Jg. 11, Heft 1, 1955, pp. 12ff.

Idem, *F.C.Oetinger und die Kabbala*, in: *Judaica*, Vol. 4, 1948, pp. 268ff.

Idem, *Schelling und die Kabbala*, in: *Judaica*, Vol. 13, pp. 65-99, 143-170, 210-232.

Tholuck, *De ortu Cabbalae*, (Hamburg: 1837).

Lutterbeck, G.A., *Die neutestamentlichen Lehrbegriffe*, Vol. 1, 1853.

Older literature that deals with problems and themes of the Christian Kabbalah:
Buddeus, J.F., *Introductio ad historiam philosophiae Hebraeorum*, (Halle: 1702 and 1721).

Kleuker, J.F., *Über die Natur und den Ursprung der Emanationslehre bei den Kabbalisten*, (Riga: 1786).

Wachter, J.G., *Der Spinozismus im Judentum oder die von dem heutigen Judentum und dessen geheimer Kabbala vergötterte Welt*, (Amsterdam: 1699).

Idem, *Elucidarius cabbalisticus sive reconditae Ebraeorum philosophiae brevis recensio*, (Rome: 1706).

Reimmann, Jac. Fr., *Einleitung zur Historie der Theologie insgemein und der jüdischen insbesondere*, (Magdeburg: 1717).

A history of the Christian Kabbalists has not been written until recently. The only one that, up to this point, has listed the most important representatives of the Christian Kabbalists is Hamberger, in his article cited above. He names: Reuchlin, the Buxtorfs, Rittangel, Hottinger, Athanasius Kircher, Vitringa, Knorr von Rosenroth, H.More, Buddeus, Kleuker, Schelling, Franz von Baader, Friedrich von Meyer, Joseph Franz Molitor and Adolph Koester.

2. The works of W.A.Schultze on Boehme and the Kabbalah (see bibliography in note 1) contain, unfortunately, no evidence for Jacob Boehme's sources. John Joseph Stoudt in his excellent work: *Sunrise to Eternity, A Study in Jacob Boehme's Life and Thought*, (Philadelphia: 1967), points to the possibility that Boehme was acquainted with the writings of Reuchlin. "During this period knowledge of the Cabala was not unusual. Reuchlin's works were available for those unable to read Hebrew, and it was not hard to find someone who had read him. Agrippa von Nettesheim and Paracelsus were also well known. In his later works Boehme even used the word Cabala twice (*Theos.Frag.* III, 34; VI,11)." Boehme himself did not know Latin. Even so, he could have obtained his knowledge of the Kabbalah through Jewish and learned Christian intermediaries.

3. His work, *Septuaginta duae conclusions cabbalisticae* appeared in 1486.

4. Scholem, Gershom, *Zur Geschichte der Anfänge der christlichen Kabbala*, Tribute to Leo Baeck, 1954.

5. Idem, pp. 166ff.; Cassuto, "Wer war der Orientalist Mithridates?" in: *Zeitschr. D. Geschichte der Juden in Deutschland*, Vol. V, 1934, pp. 230-236.

6. Scholem, *Anfänge*, p. 170.

7. Cf. Baer, *Abner aus Burgos, Korrespondenzblatt des Vereins zur Gr̦ndung einer Akademie,* 1925, pp. 20-37.

8. Ibid, p. 33.

9. On Raimundus Lullus, see Zwemer, Samuel M., *Rayund Lull, First Missionary to the Moslems,* New York, Chicago, Toronto 1902; Guttmann, I., *Die Scholastik des 13 Jahrhunderts in ihren Beziehungen zum Judentum,* 1902, pp. 150 ff.

10. Scholem, *Anfänge,* p.171.

11. Ibid, p. 79.

12. Ibid, p. 188.

13. On Reuchlin, see Geiger, Ludwig, *Joh.Reuchlin, Sein Leben und seine Werke,* Lepizig 1871; idem, *Joh.Reuchlin, Briefwechsel,* Tübingen 1875 (= Publ. D. Stuttgarter Vereins). Geiger's view emerges from his article, Reuchlin in ADB, vol. 28, p. 793, where he says of the Kabbalistic works of Reuchlin, that they may be considered "today more than the product of a sick mind because they are the result of genuine philosophical research." See also the article by Kawerau, G. on Reuchlin, RE, vol. 16, p. 681ff. See also Peuckert, Will-Erich, *Pansophie,* (Stuttgart: 1936), pp. 113ff, 122ff.

14. See the essay by Rocholl, *Zeitschrift für Kirchengeschichte,* Vol. 13, pp. 84ff.

15. Ehmann, Karl Chr.F., *C.F.Oetingers Leben und Briefe,* (Stuttgart: 1859), p. 50.

16. See Scholem, Gershom, *Jüdische Mystik in ihren Hauptströmungen,* (Zürich: 1957). On Abarbanel, see c. III: "Hasidism in mediaeval Germany," (New York: 1946), pp. 80ff.

17. See Guttmann, I., *Die religionsphilosophischen Lehren des Don Isaak Abravanel,* 1916. On Leone Ebreo, seee *Dialoghi d'Amore a cura di Santino Caramella,* (Bari: 1929).

18. See Müller, Ernst, *Der Seher und seine Lehre,* 1923; Scholem, *Trends,* pp. 156ff.

19. Eccl. 1.4: Prior omnibus creata est Sapientia [Wisdom was created before all things].

20. *Oetingers Selbstbiographie,* (Gmünd: 1927), p. 29.

21. Theologia ex idea vitae deducta, p. XXVII: "Corpus internum gloriae Dei, sui manifestativae, competere, centena scripturae loca clamant sed sic habeto: corpus hoc nullam admittere limitationem, ut in Cabala denudata falso ab illuminatissimo

Iizschak Lorja demonstratur, qui statuit causam supremam Deum, unicum sibi simillimum habere causatum logos, qui es Adam Kadmon. Id sane Arianismum genuit, cum statuit hoc causatum esse, quid limitatum et contingens."

22. Johann Jakob Schütz has written a number of edifying works: *Christliches Gedenkbüchlein zur Beförderung eines anfangenden neuen Lebens*, 1675; *Christliche Lebensregeln*, 1677. See ADB XXXIII, pp. 129ff.; H. Dechent in, *Christliche Welt*, 1889, nos. 43, 44, 47, 48.

23. Cf. Salecker, Kurt, "Christian Knorr von Rosenroth" in, *Palaestra* 178, (Leipzig: 1931).

24. An especially important work by him is *Coniectura Cabbalistica* or *A Conjectural Essay of Interpreting the mind of Moses according to a Threefold Cabbala, viz.: Literal, Philosophical, Mystical or Divinely Moral*, 1653, dedicated to his brother Platonist, R.Cudworth.

25. See note 23.

26. "Explicat ambigua utroque in Foedere sensus.
Alta videt, denoque notat cognomina Trinum
Lucens pneumatice, paganas discutit umbras
Edomat internos quos spumat Passio Fluctus.
Alterat abstrusos minerarum in corde meatus
Intrat in Arcana et secreta palatial lustrat."

27. Knorr von Rosenroth, *Cabbala Denudata*, apparatus in librum Sohar, pars secunda, p. 3.

28. Ibid, Book I, part II, p. 177: "Equidem studium tuum atque solicitudinem de convertendis Judaeis magnopere laudo, quippe opus dignum viro non nomine solum, sed et re ipsa Christiano. Tuaeque sententiae accedo, quod non solum utile sed fere necessarium sit, antequam res tanti momenti suscipiatur, ut Christianus ac Judaeus mutuam utriusque intelligant Theologiam sive Theosophiam. Ac proinde quod non contemnendum gradum ad hanc rem faciat, qui se communem utriusque praestat Interpretem. Qua de causa ingentes profecto tibi debentur gratiae non tantum a re publica literaria, sed a toto Christiano orbe, quod hanc tam difficilem Provinciam in te susceperis."

29. Ibid: "Tum denique quod praecipua laudatissimi tui Instituti pars non tam eo collineat ut unam certam integramque Cabbalam, ex his ruderibus Judaicis extruas, quam ut Judaei et Christiani

suam utriusque Theosophiam mutuo intelligant libereque quid solidum quidve secus utrobique reperiatur, apud se ipsos perpendant."

30. Ibid, p. 4: "Ipse quoque libri stylus mirum quantum conducit ad meliorem multarum Phrasium Novi foederis intellectum."

31. Ibid, p. 5. He gives for that reason the express hope, "ab ipsius Regni Christi temporibus similia studia non fore aliena."

32. When August Wünsche concludes his article on the Kabbalah in the *Realenzyklopaedie für prot.Theologie und Kirche*, Vol. 9, p. 689, with the words: "The doctrine of Christ the God-man in no way parallels the confused doctrine of Adam Kadmon, the pre-worldly, spiritual Primordial Man," then he indicates that modern New Testament scholarship nevertheless has demonstrated that not only the Johannine vision of the Logos, but also the vision of the Son of Man underlies the presentation of the heavenly Primordial Man, in which the early Christian doctrine of the Logos and the early Christian understanding of the messianic Son of Man was shaped.

33. Francofurti ad Moenum, Sumtu Johannis Davidis Zunneri, Cassitero Joh.Phil.Andreae, Anno MDCLXXXIV.

34. See Salecker, Kurt, *Christian Knorr von Rosenroth*, p. 12.

35. Rommel, Chr.v., *Leibniz und Landgraf Ernst*, (Frankfurt: 1847), Vol. II, p. 123.

36. G.G.Leibnitii, *Opera omnia*, ed. Dutens, p. 92.

37. See Salecker, p. 12.

38. See Salecker, p. 12.

39. Salecker, p. 13; Ehmann, *Leben und Briefe*, p. 59. Oetinger's quote of Plato here is taken from Franciscus Patricius, *Mystica Egyptiorum*, lib. 1, c. 4: "Agnovi me esse partem mundi superioris, adeptusque vitam aeternam sub luce incogitabili; sed lassitudine delapsus ab ista contemplatione intellectus puri ad imaginationem, lux illa me deseruit." He mentions this trip of Plato in the higher world also in a letter to the duchess of Gotha, dated September 1763, when he presented his most significant Kabbalistic work, "Lehrtafel der Prinzessin Antonia," to the duchess. See Ehmann, *Leben und Briefe*, no. 521, p. 662f. "Your most Serene Highness. I present to your enlightened eyes the muse and counterpart of sublime literature. This is the font from which Plato drew his highest inspiration. We are

quite insignificant compared to Plato. He made once a journey to the intelligible world above, and afterwards he lamented his return to the realm of imagination. Princess Antonia sought to raise herself to a flight above imagination, but it is not possible to judge whether or not she reached her goal. As an admirer of your illumined personage, I am happy to offer to you this work." Ehmann, *Leben und Briefe*, p. 612, from the letters of Oetinger to the count of Castell, in the year 1756, no. 378: "From *Peganius*, i.e. Baron Rosenroth, I drew a statement that God does not allow himself to be seen by his creatures, except in a Shekinah or dwelling that creatures can endure. Therefore, outside of the Lamb (Rev 4) God appears in iridescence as well as in a Shekinah. The Lamb, however, appears in a special way.

To be sure, Christ alone is the true dwelling place and Shekinah of God, and I know only to refer the revelation of God in Christ to the near fulfillment of the mystery of God and Christ. It would be enough to demonstrate that what we call heaven is but a middle point, and that very many stand on the two sides. (He refers to his *Leichen-Carmen* on the intermediate state, which he made on the death of his son, Carl Martin, who died on November 11, 1752 in Weinsberg.)

40. The idea that Plato was a student of the prophet Jeremiah was already expressed in Philo of Alexandria and was repeatedly discussed in all the centuries up to Pico de la Mirandola and Reuchlin.

41. Scholem, *Jüdische Mystik*, p. 260.

42. Sulzbach 1684. see Salecker, K., p. 45, and Schoeps, Hans-Joachim, *Philosemitismus im Barock*, (Tübingen: 1952), p. 80.

43. See Schoeps, p. 80.

44. Ehmann, *Leben und Briefe*, p. 58.

45. Ibid, p. 60.

46. Ibid, p. 64.

47. *Aufmunternde Gründe zu Lesung der Schriften Jakob Boehmes*, (Frankfurt und Leipzig: 1731), c. 1, ß16, p. 258.

48. See Scholem, *Jüdische Mystik*, p. 267.

49. Ehmann, *Leben und Briefe*, pp. 629f.

50. An explanation of the public document of the Master Tablet engraved in copper by the late Princess Antonia of Wirtemberg, whose original she made from the magnificent painting of the

ten mirrored-splendors of God at the Deinach Fountain, together with an explanation of the power of the fountain sources, of the philosophy of the Hebrews, and in general of the Spirit of God according to all passages of the New Testament, is given by M. Friedrich Christoph Oetinger, in: *F.C.Oetinger, Sämmtl.Schriften*, hg. Von Karl Chr.E.Ehmann, 2. Abth., Vol. 1, (Stuttgart: 1858). Oetinger mentions the Master Tablet frequently in his correspondence, as he does for example in his letter to the Count of Castell (Letter no. 515 in Ehmann, *Leben und Briefe*, p. 657). "Thus, E.Exc. will have received my plan regarding the Sefiroth of the Jews. I maintain that John wrote in the style of the Kabbalists. My next completed book will show what a scribe must do to find words that come from pure sources. It is remarkable that my book, *Antonia*, passed the censor. Two publications of it cost me 80 copper Gulden. In it, the philosophies, including the philosophy of *sans souci*, are compared." To the same Count he wrote in 1764 (Letter no. 536, Ehmann, *Leben und Briefe*, p. 671): "Ach! If I could I would tell princes and great lords what they should plant for posterity in preparation for the brotherhood [Philadelphia] of the Jews. No wonder that I prefer E.Exc. I would also like to send the book, *Antonia*, to the Duke of Meklenburg and the King of England and the Czar, and take a chance, as it were. Risum teneatis amici!"

51. Oetinger, F.C., *Sämtl.Predigten*, ed. by Karl E. Ehmann, Vol. 4, (Reutlingen: 1856), p. 328.

52. Pico, *opera omnia*, (Basel: 1557), p. 105; see Scholem, *Anfänge*, p. 169. Oetinger, *Beurtheilungen der wichtigen Lehre von dem Zustand nach dem Tod.Sämmtl.Schriften*, II. Abth., Vol. 6, p. 220.

Oetinger speaks on the permanence of revelation in the Church:

"Almost at the same time (as the prophet Hans Engelbrecht of Brunswick), i J. 1623, God awakened Princess Antonia of Wurtemberg in another way. She was the sister of Duke Eberhard III. She donated a public Tablet at the mineral springs of Deinach. Her writings, in which she explains the Tablet, ought to have been printed by the Censor of the Consistorium. However, one it is not worth the trouble to dwell on these things, although she brings clearly to light the writing's sound wisdom for theology." This book came out in the year 1771.

53. See Benz, Ernst, *Schellings theologische Geistesahnen*, Akademie d. Wissenschaften u. d. Literature in Mainz, Abhandl. Der geistes- und sozialwissenschaftl. Klasse, Jg. 1955, Nr. 3, (Wiesbaden: 1955), pp. 47ff.
Knorr von Rosenroth included the doctrine of the ten Sefiroth in a poem in his "Neuer Helikon" and concluded the "100 Words of Praise" with their enumeration:
"To you alone belong the Crown, Wisdom and Teaching, Eternally art Thou honored as gentle and strong and beautiful. To Thee art victory, praise, earth, the Kingdom subject. Make, form and create us aright and flow in us eternally!" ("Neuer Helikon," *Geistliches Lustspiel*, p. 254.)
Oetinger, *Auszug aus der Herzenstheologie vom Geheimnis Gottes und Christi, Sämmtl.Schriften*, II. Abth., Vol. 6, p. 306: "God's Being consists in the manifestatio sui (self-manifestation), in the emanation of himself. This is the ancient Kabbalistic and Wisdom doctrine, and Jacob Boehme certainly speaks of it. The name Jehovah exists in the revelation to Israel, and the name Elohim in the revelation in the clouds or nature (Ps. 68.35). And whoever knows the revealed name Jehovah, to him the spiritual and bodily elements are subject. Now, since the fullness of divinity has been revealed bodily in Christ, then must also all things be revealed bodily to the community of Christ, as to his body."
54. Meanwhile, the essay on Schelling and the Kabbalah mentioned in note 1 has appeared by W.A.Schulze, which refers to the same connections.
55. Benz, *Schellings theologische Geistesahnen*, p. 278ff.
56. *Lehrtafel*, p. 88.
57. Ibid, p. 29.
58. Ibid, pp. 133, 134.
59. Ibid, p. 171; see also Oetinger, *Aufmunternde Gründe*.
60. Benz, Ernst, *Schellings theologische Geistesahnen*, p. 279.
61. Oetinger, *Irrd. u. himml. Philos.*, p. 341. See also the chptr, "Leiblichkeit" in Auberle, C.A., *Die Theosophie F. Chr. Oetingers*, Tübingen 1847, p. 147ff.
62. *Lehrtafel*, p. 393.
63. In this second book, evidence is found, with the help of the Kabbalistic speculation on letters, that the entire Christian

doctrine of the Trinity is contained already in the second word of the Creation account, "bara" ("create"), since the letter 'b' refers to *ben*, the Son, the letter 'r' to *ruach*, the Holy Spirit, and the letter a to *ab* ("Father").

64. On this, refer to Oetinger, *Himmlische und irrdische Philosophie Swedenborgs*, p. 343.

65. *Lehrtafel*, p. 123.

66. Ibid, p. 36.

67. *Emblem. Wörterbuch*, p. 535. see also Auberle, C.A., *Die Theosophie F. Chr. Oetingers nach ihren Grundzügen*, (Tübingen: 1847), and his criticism of Oetinger's doctrine of the Trinity, p. 163f.

68. *Lehrtafel*, p. 394.

69. Oetinger, *Himml. und Ird. Philosophie Swedenborgs*, Part II, p. 324."When the Mirrored-splendors of GOd are outflowing toward the creature they are called the seven Spirits of GOd. But when they remain within GOd they are called the Word from the Beginning. In themselves, the seven Spirits of GOd are simply a mirrored-splendor. The Mirrored-splendors of GOd are called Sefiroth by the Jews. In this way, they intend to explain what constitutes the fullness of the Godhead. There are ten Sefiroth. Rhenferd divides them into the "haeljonoth" Sefiroth and the "hatachtonjot" Sefiroth. These outflow together with the holy Greeting from him who is, who was and who will be, and from the seven Spirits. The three upper Sefiroth are the Trinity of which the ancient Jews held very important ideas. As one can see from Herr Sommers *Specimine Theologiae Soharicae*, p. 61, the seven lower Sefiroth are the seven Spirits of GOd. They are uncreated, being eternal mirrored-emanations of God; but they nevertheless take on themselves a creaturely mass, whereas the three upper [Sefiroth] have in themselves no creaturely mass, but are rather pure Light and Understanding in their Being and Essence. Nevertheless, they give to the three upper [Sefiroth] that subsistence which belongs to incommunicability; in other words, each of the three is said to be above any of the other [lower Sefiroth]. On this, I could adduce many passages from the most learned Jews, but I will save that for another time. For now, I will simply say that Father, Son and Spirit exist in each other; that is to say, none can exist without the others. That is

why the Three can be One, not enumerating them in any kind of arithmetical sense, but as JEsus says: 'I and the Father are One,' and John 17, 'that they all may be One.' In this manner the seven all are in one another, and therefore each of the seven possesses a power that is uniquely its own. The very ancient Jews, such as Rabbi Joseph and Rabbi Simeon ben Jochai, designated the seven lower Sefiroth with these names: Gedulah [or Chesed], Gevurah [Din], Tiphereth, Netsah, Hod, Yesod, Malkuth."

70. Ibid, p. 325.
71. Ziegler, Leopold, *Das Lehrgespräch vom Allgemeinen Menschen*, (Hamburg: 1956), p. 186.

The KEY
to the KABBALISTIC Master Tablet
of Princess Antonia of Würtemberg
IN THE CHURCH OF THE TRINITY IN DEINACH

Including the ten Sefiroth or Emanations of God: a: God the Father, b. God the Son, c. God the Holy Spirit, d. Grace, e. Righteousness, f. Love, g. Victory, h. Praise, i. the Fundament, k. Christ, l. Ruben, m. Simon, n. Levi, o. Judah, p. Zebulon, q. Isachar, r. Dan, s. Gad, t. Asher, u. Naphtali, x. Joseph, y. Benjamin.

1.   The Crown of the Kingdom; under that, the monogram   of Princess Antonia, surrounded by the wreath of the   palms of victory.
2.   The 24 most ancients.
3.   Elijah with the sword.
4.   Moses in the burning bush.
5.   Enoch with a book.
6.   The battle and victory of Michael.
7.   The Lamb from Zion.
8.   Overthrow of the dragon.
9.   Company of the saints around Mt. Zion.
10.   Angels singing praises.
11.   Angel with palm branch.
12.   God, as judge, with the saints.
13.   Ascension of Christ.
14.   Outpouring of the Spirit.
15.   Wheels of Ezekiel.
16.   Four Beasts of Ezekiel.
17.   Transfiguration of Jesus on the Mountain.
18.   Woman washing Jesus' feet.
19.   Birth of Jesus.
20.   Prodigal Son.
21.   Angel with Mary.
22.   Jesus teaching in the Temple.
23.   Element of fire.
24.   Element of water.
25.   Elijah's ascent to heaven.
26.   Jonah swallowed by the whale.
27.   The three men in the fiery furnace.
28.   The baptism of Jesus.
29.   Solomon's wise judgment.
30.   Esther comes to King Ahasuerus
31.   Abraham intending to sacrifice his son, Isaac.
32.   David coming to eat the Bread of the Presence when on his flight.
33.   Agag slain by Samuel.
34.   The young Tobias led by Raphael.
35.   Jacob wrestles with God.

36. Jacob sees the ladder to heaven in a dream.
37. Victories against Amalek.
38. Daniel's handwriting on the wall.
39. Gideon's victory over the Midianites in the encampment.
40. Lot saved by Abraham.
41. Pharaoh and his entire army drowning in the Red Sea.
42. Gideon determines from how they drink the water which of the Israelites should go with him into battle.
43. Jesus speaks with the Samaritan woman at Jacob's well.
44. Noah's ark.
45. Daniel's vision of the kingdoms of metal.
46. The angel swearing to the perfection of the mysteries of God.
47. Mt. Sinai covered in smoke.
48. Mt. Zion.
49. The Israelite's encampment with the Tabernacle.
50. The City of Jerusalem.
51. The Angel with the millstone in the *Apocalypse*.
52. The Angel with the eternal Gospel.
53. The bronze serpent.
54. Jesus crucified.
55. John the Baptist.
56. Moses with the Law.
57. Joshua.
58. Paul, apostle to the Gentiles.
59. Aaron behind the altar of sacrifice.
60. Adam and Eve expelled from Paradise.
61. Hezekiah becomes aware of the sundial going backward.
62. The God of Israel answering Elijah with fire.
63. Manna falling from heaven.
64. Sampson slaughters a lion.
65. Joseph explaining the two dreams.
66. Christ's cup of suffering on the Mount of Olives.

67. The fateful cup in Benjamin's sack.
68. Lazarus' sores being licked by dogs.
69. The Good Samaritan.
70. Elijah fed by the angel.
71. Jesus feeding the people in the Wilderness.
72. Entombment of Jesus.
73. Resurrection of Jesus.
74. Jacob blessing the two sons of Joseph.
75. Jesus welcoming the children and blessing them.
76. Circumcision.
77. The child, Jesus, being brought to the temple.
78. The Arabian Queen coming to Solomon.
79. The Magi from the East coming to Christ.
80. David's victory will be envied.
81. David overcoming Goliath.
82. David bringing the Ark of the Covenant home.
83. Jesus entering Jerusalem.
84. Martha and Mary.
85. Jesus anointed by the woman and betrayed by Judas.
86. Jacob buried behind the hill of Machpela.
87. Lazarus coming out of the tomb.
88. The four great prophets.
89. The four Evangelists.
90. The twelve minor prophets.
91. The 12 apostles.

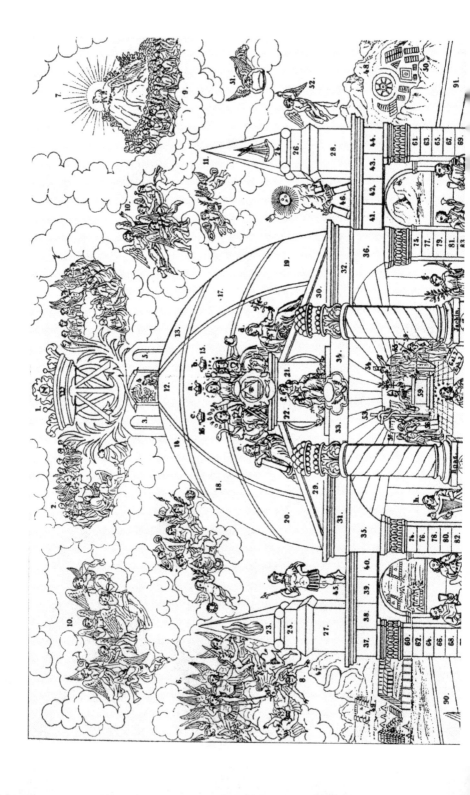

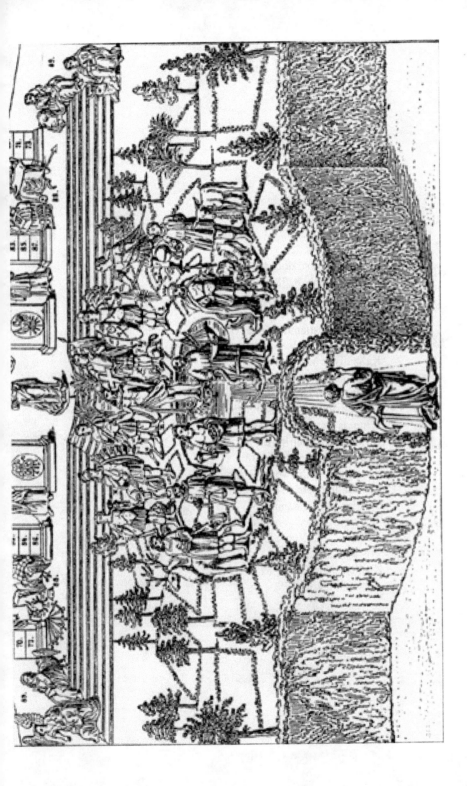

Index

Printed in the USA
CPSIA information can be obtained
at www.ICGtesting.com
LVHW022346290124
770282LV00010B/527